S0-AYB-284

Spiritual Partners

Spiritual Partners
Profiles in Creative Marriage

Cornelia Jessey and Irving Sussman

CROSSROAD · NEW YORK

1982

The Crossroad Publishing Company
575 Lexington Avenue, New York, NY 10022

Copyright © 1982 by Cornelia Jessey and Irving Sussman

All rights reserved. No part of this book may be reproduced, stored in a re-
trieval system, or transmitted, in any form or by any means, electronic, me-
chanical, photocopying, recording, or otherwise, without the written permission
of The Crossroad Publishing Company.

Printed in the United States of America

Library of Congress Cataloging in Publication Data

Sussman, Cornelia.
    Spiritual partners.

    Bibliography: p.
    Includes index.
    Contents: Catherine and William Blake—Frances and
Gilbert Chesterton—Maisie Ward and Frank Sheed—
[etc.]
    1. Marriage—Case studies.   2. Intellectuals—Case
studies.   I. Sussman, Irving.   II. Title.
HQ518.S85   306.8   81-22069
ISBN 0-8245-0438-0   AACR2

HQ 518
.J58

GESW

To Simon

Not yet, O Hill! high hill of Autumn scatter
Red leaves and gold athwart the distant view.
Let me gaze on, a little instant longer,
Where she I love leans toward me through the blue!
—Hitomaro, "On Parting from his Wife"
(Japan, ca. 70 A.D.)

Among warblers, the males who sing the widest repertoire of syllables also attract mates soonest. Intriguingly, this is only true of the monogamous species of warbler. Species in which the male mates with many females have a very poor song repertoire.
—*The Economist*

Contents

ACKNOWLEDGMENTS

The authors gratefully acknowledge the generous benefits of the thoughts, commentaries, and memories of friends who had personally known many of the couples in these chapters. Some had known Gilbert and Frances Chesterton or heard Gilbert Chesterton lecture in the United States on his second visit to America in the early thirties. We ourselves met the Bubers and heard Martin Buber lecture in 1958 just before Paula died. The same is true for the Maritains—to whom we were introduced by Msgr. John M. Oesterreicher when we wrote for his series called *The Bridge,* for which Raissa Maritain also wrote. Later, after Raissa's death, we knew Jacques Maritain personally through John Howard Griffin and the historic visit to Gethsemani to see Thomas Merton. Lanza del Vasto (Shantidas), through his own kindness and the generosity of his secretary, Yvette Naal, personally assisted us with biographical material in the chapter on Shantidas and Chanterelle.

We express our thanks most particularly to Fr. Simon Scanlon, OFM, editor of *Way*, and to *Way* magazine for encouraging us to write many of these essays, in somewhat different versions, and for giving us all rights. And we thank our present editor, Caroline Whiting, for befriending the manuscript.

Prologue One

Playing the numbers game has been for centuries the method by which emperors, politicians, and merchants have measured success or failure. Napoleon claimed great victory if 100,000 of the enemy were found dead on the battlefield and only 50,000 Frenchmen were killed in the encounter; a president of the United States claimed a landslide victory and a mandate from *all* the people even though 17 percent of the voting population bothered to go to the polls, while 83 percent refused to vote for him or anyone else. Merchants, banks, conglomerates, and multinational oil cartels figure success not by mere profit, but by maximum profits plus. The game is played by the newsmedia to a rather insensitive degree: a disaster is categorized by the cost of the property destroyed—"The loss to the structure in the hotel explosion is estimated to be in the millions and is considered a major disaster." That report went on to state that the loss in human lives was less than it might have been—"It is fortunate that only nine lives were lost, and only seventy injured, some seriously"—and, therefore, the disaster was not a major one!

For a long time now the numbers game has found its place of honor among psychologists, sociologists, pollsters, and religious moralists. The numbers used to show the success or failure of marriages vary. One of the largest figures quoted estimates that 30 percent of all marriages end in divorce. The statistic strikes apprehension in society's soul: Isn't it clear that if 30 percent of all marriages end in divorce, marriages are on the way out, along with that other atavism, romantic love? Furthermore, doesn't that 30 percent show that man is by nature polygamous?

The statistic is never given the other way around; no one says, "70 percent of all marriages last for a lifetime." The 30 percent figure gets the attention just as the squeaking wheel gets the grease.

The couples written about in this book were married for life; statistics, theories, philosophies about monogamy or polygamy did not concern them. This does not mean they took their marriages for granted. On the contrary, they were creative artists who made an art of marriage without thinking of themselves as role models for happy marriages. They undertook marriage as a creative adventure, a dare, and a responsibility. They did not make, as Elizabeth Barrett made for Robert Browning, lists counting the ways they loved, nor did they give reasons for loving each other. Their creative work and their holistic marriages partook of a oneness so that marriage, monogamy, creativity, and responsibility could not be distinguished one from another.

In writing this book we put aside any preconceived ideas about the lives or works or marriages of the couples; nor did we take as gospel what critics and writers said of them or their work. Our chief concern was to observe what was there and let that speak to the purpose. We were granted the privilege of meeting personally Raissa and Jacques Maritain, of hearing G. K. Chesterton lecture, of talking with relatives and friends of Martin and Paula Buber, and of hearing Shantidas himself praise his and Chanterelle's story as spiritually and factually truthful. Cyril Clemens, editor of the *Mark Twain Journal,* read and highly approved of the essay on his kinsman, Samuel Clemens. As for the others discussed in this book, their creative lives were related to us through original sources and not through what others conjectured.

We wrote about these couples not because we agreed or disagreed with theories about monogamy or polygamy; we wrote about them because the profiles of their monogamous marriages make such darn good stories.

Prologue Two

From Prologue One, it may be evident that this is and is not a "marriage book." It is not about the way to have a monogamous marriage. Nor is it about the troubles of families in our time. (Families are no more troubled in our time than in any other time.) These biographies are not of couples who exemplify the pattern for an enduring marriage.

What are these monogamous marriage stories, then? They are the stories of romantic lovers who seemed predestined to come together in order to bring forth a creative work, not their children—though many had children—but a contribution to Western civilization and culture.

All of these monogamous couples were famous people, but not famous for their marriages. They were famous for the work produced out of their having come together. Each person, as a partner in the marriage, and also each pair, was different from the other persons and from the other pairs. Yet all had certain things in common. The most striking thing is that all were romantics.

For example, when Samuel Clemens (Mark Twain) met the semi-invalid Olivia, they tested each other's existence with a kiss. The writer was already famous, but mostly for his ribald, sardonic

3

humor and dark commentary on the human race. He entered into his love-marriage as a virgin of thirty-four. Monogamy was the rule in their time—socially, politically, and economically. But Sam and Olivia would have been monogamous had they lived in polygamous Mormonia. There are many different kinds of monogamy.

For centuries the *idea* of the indissolubility of marriage was a spiritually powerful shaping force in Judeo-Christian Western culture. Our civilization is formed by this *idea*. But monogamous marriages were more pragmatic than spiritual. For political, ruling families, the monogamous marriage was arranged, usually in the interests of national security. For middle-class families—down to the mid-twentieth century—monogamy was often arranged for the sake of property and inheritance security, as well as for safeguarding women and children.

At the same time, the other kind of monogamy, dictated by romantic love, was common. The two kinds came together often; for example, in the relationship of Elizabeth of Hungary and Louis of Thuringia in the Middle Ages. Their marriage, arranged in childhood for reasons of state, turned into a famous love story, which produced an amazing creative work—born of Elizabeth, but impossible without the fertilizing spirit of Louis. It was a creative work for humanity—Elizabeth founded hospitals—and brought a further dimension to the significance of romantic love—she was sainted.

The couples whose monogamous marriages are presented in this book have similarities—all of them fell in love romantically, and all produced a particularly meaningful creative work that influenced our civilization and contributed to our culture. Such married couples may not seem to have much in common with the general lot of couples. Yet, they were human. They lived out the vision that is most common among lovers—the dream of romantic love that endures. And their task—that of relating to each other, with each one's vast differences from the other, the responsibility each offered the other—is the common task. Their marriages reveal how life-engrossing is the work of making a reality together. Reality is, in truth, their contribution—their dimension of reality is what they gave to the world. Ultimately, all marriages seek to make just that: a reality.

It may seem, on first considering such monogamous couples, that they are very rare. However, there are so many, down through the centuries, that we had a hard time picking and choosing which marriages to write about.

We had to leave out not only Louis of Thuringia and Elizabeth of Hungary, but also John and Anne Donne, Léon Bloy and Jeanne Molbech ("In one brief meeting two destinies were sealed"), C. S. (Clive Stapes) Lewis and Joy Davidman, Padraic and Mary Colum, John Howard and Elizabeth Griffin, the Stravinskys, Joseph and Sally Cunneen, José and Catherine de Vinck, Peter and Linda Sabbath, Charles and Anne Lindbergh, William Carlos and Florence (Floss) Williams, and many, many more.

The couples we chose begin with Catherine and William Blake.

I

Catherine and William Blake

Wiliam Blake had visions, some of which came to him and never left him; others were like flashes of light that brilliantly illuminate only to fade almost immediately. One vision that never left, but became the focus of his poetry, his art, his creative marriage, was the vision of a New Jerusalem rising phoenix-like from the ashes of a burnt-out England. He saw England being completely consumed because of man's inhumanity to man, cruelty to children and animals, indifference to doing what is realistic, responsible, and right.

However, Blake's visions found as little respect among social philosophers, establishment-religious, and successful poets as did his great paintings and engravings among the more prosperous artists and writers whose "products" sold so successfully in the London marketplaces.

William Blake died in the year 1827, so dire his poverty there was not enough money to pay for a plot of ground in which to bury him. It was not until 1927 that he began to be recognized and appreciated as the forerunner of the "romantic movement" in poetry, as a consummate artist-philosopher, as the founder of the expressionists in painting, as the prophet of modernism in art. It was through the love and efforts of Yeats, Swinburne, Rossetti, and Shaw, one hundred years after Blake's death, that recognition came to one of England's great visionary and creative artists.

Had such recognition come during their lifetimes, William and Catherine Blake would have been sorry about it rather than pleased. In his last illness he told her, "I should be sorry if I had any earthly fame. I wish to do nothing for profit. I wish to live for art. I am quite happy."[1] But, if his work was unrecognized during his lifetime, his marriage to Catherine Boucher was recognized, admired, and thought perfect by almost everyone who knew them. "The name of Catherine Blake is destined to go down in the minds and hearts of posterity as that of an almost perfect wife," wrote Geoffrey Langdon Keynes, the foremost student of and authority on the life of the Blakes.

One should envision the love of Romeo and Juliet as not being star-crossed or death-marked to imagine the love of the Blakes for each other. As with Shakespeare's lovers, William and Catherine were drawn together by a *command* of love and monogamous marriage. Their marriage was "a marriage of the New Adam and Eve in a New Jerusalem . . . and *this* is Jerusalem in every man: A tent and a tabernacle of mutual forgiveness." This New Jerusalem was real; it came as an actuality at a specific date, 1757, William Blake's birthdate. It came out of "the forests of the night" and would become a real City, where "Heaven, Earth, and Hell henceforth shall live in harmony."

The New Adam and Eve did not spring from the roots planted in the pristine Garden of Eden; the New Adam and Eve in this New Jerusalem was a fresh flowering. Roots did not concern William Blake. He wrote:

> The rat, the mouse, the fox, the rabbit watch the roots;
> the lion, the tiger, the horse, the elephant watch the fruits.[2]

Little is known about William Blake's roots. He was born in London at 28 Broad Street, Golden Square, on November 28, 1757. William's father, James, was a poor hosier. At his shop patrons and neighbors met, sometimes to transact business, but mostly to discuss and argue the news of the day, the politics and, above all, the philosophy, religion, and prophecies of Emanuel Swedenborg. Swedenborg was an influential Swedish scientist-philosopher whose writings were then the rage in England, as in most of Europe. His most influential book, *Heaven and Hell,* was replacing even the Bible as a topic for religious discussion and became the hottest topic in the shop during William's childhood.

One of the prophecies of Swedenborg lent an element of mystery, a touch of piquancy, to the discussions that took place in the shop on Broad Street. Swedenborg had written that in his visions and dreams, in his conversations with the spirits of the Hebrew prophets, God had revealed to him that in the year 1757 (he wrote down the vision in 1740) the Old World would end and the New World begin. From that day forward the old theologies would be "rolled up like a scroll" and the New Jerusalem would come upon the earth.

The child born on that prophetic date, William Blake, was at times the main topic of discussion. As he grew older he heard and thought about the prophecy, impressed by the prediction of a spiritual and humanitarian revolution beginning on the date of his birth. It affected his behavior, his outlook on persons and nature, and it set him apart from his brothers and sisters. He was a strange blossom on a most ordinary family tree. His father was more sympathetic and understanding of his strange behavior than was his mother, although both he and his wife favored the oldest son, John, who turned out to be the black sheep of the family. Perhaps it was the coincidence of William's having been born on the prophetic day, or perhaps it was that he recognized how different this son was from his other children—John, James, Robert, and a daughter. Whatever the reason, William's father put no restraints on his son's supernaturally active imagination.

Uncertain what should be done about his son's education, James Blake decided to make a painter of him. He took William to an engraver's studio, to a man by the name of Rylands, who was at the summit of popularity with the London booksellers. Rylands accepted the young William, recognizing from some of the samples of the boy's drawings that the lad had possibilities. However, after the first day with Rylands, William walked away from the studio and came home. His father, annoyed and angered, reprimanded him: "You have left the finest engraver in the City! You must go back!" William stood firm: "Father, I do not like the man's looks; he looks as if he would live to be hanged."

It is the first recorded prophecy of William Blake, made while he was yet a young boy, and it came true. Twelve years later, Rylands was hanged for forgery. It was the first prophecy William Blake uttered, but it was not the first of his visions, which came to him from earliest childhood. He was only four when one day, looking out through the casement, he suddenly saw "God put His forehead to the window." He set up a loud scream that brought his mother running into the room. She controlled her temper that time and let him off with a scolding for "making up such an unlikely story." At other times he did not escape a beating, as on the day he stayed out in the fields of Peckham Rye longer than was permitted. He explained that he was late because as he passed a tree full of angels, "their bright wings shining among the boughs," he stayed to watch and talk with them. He went on to say that while he was wandering in the fields he found Ezekiel sitting in the warm summer sun, there in the open fields. He got more than a mere scolding from his mother.

Visions came to William Blake for the rest of his life, sometimes with such overwhelming rapidity and brilliance he could not write them all down. They went far beyond what Swedenborg had seen. The New Jerusalem Blake saw was a reality in which he was a New Adam with a New Eve. He with his Eve would be like that one grain of sand in Lambeth, that one grain of sand which Satan could not find. In one of his visions he and his Eve were breaking bread with two of the Prophets, Isaiah and Ezekiel: "They dined with us, and I asked them how they dared so roundly to assert that God spoke to them, and whether they did not think at the time that they would be misunderstood." Isaiah answered that he did not see God, nor hear in a "finite organical perception," but that his senses discovered the infinite in everything, so that he became persuaded that the voice of honest indignation is the voice of God, "and I cared not for consequences, but wrote." The visions were so real to William that after he married Catherine, she, too, was able to see them.

There is no evidence, direct or circumstantial, to imply that Catherine Boucher, before her meeting William Blake, manifested any visionary or mystical proclivities. She was a normal, healthy, vivacious, tender-hearted young girl. The daughter of a Battersea market-gardener, she was "pretty and bright-eyed" and altogether charming. Unlike other girls of London, Catherine was not anxious to find a husband at any cost. Her mother teased her: "Catherine, dearest, whom are you going to marry?" Catherine's answer was always the same: "I have not yet seen the man." And that was that—until she laid eyes on a young, handsome, love-sick youth by the name of William Blake. William really was sick with love, but not with love for Catherine!

For a year or so before his meeting with Catherine Boucher, William, barely twenty at the time, had begun to court a girl by the name of Polly (or Clara) Woods. She was "a lovely little girl" who took walks with him here and there, and then "whistled him down the wind." She laughed at his passion for her, mocked him, teased him and took sadistic joy in telling lies about him, so that his reputation was blown about like dust in the wind. As with Shakespeare's Romeo "sinking under love's heavy burden," groaning and suffering for love of Rosaline, William Blake, with a soul of lead, was groaning and suffering for love of Polly. He followed her about hopelessly, distracted, sentimentally feeling that death was better than life without Rosaline—without Polly, that is! His love for her was ruining his health, endangering his very life. He became so ill, he was near collapse. And all the while, Polly ("she of the false smile") showed neither pity nor concern for his spiritual turmoil and physical exhaustion. He grew too weak to do much for himself, and on the advice of a physician he consented to try a change of air, not at all convinced that this, or anything else, would ease the hurt of the wound he was suffering. He was sent into the country, to Richmond, to the house of the market-gardener, Boucher, a kindly, simple man.

At first the change of environment did not seem to do much for William, who, immediately upon his arrival, plunged into telling the gardener and his wife of his agony, because of this cruel, pitiless girl. Mr. and Mrs. Boucher did not know how to comfort their love-sick guest. Then, that evening, their daughter, Catherine, entered the room unseen and stood watching and listening to the beautiful young man telling his woeful story, his animated handsome face framed with his abundant "flame-like" hair. (She would later make a drawing of him, which is the authority for the description of him.) She continued to look at him, and "grew upon the moment faint" from the intuition that she knew she was seeing her destined husband, even as Juliet knew when she first set eyes on Romeo that from then on she would "follow him throughout the world." Faint with the realization, Catherine left the room.

After a brief interval she composed herself and soon felt calm enough to reenter the room. She sat down by William, listening as he began telling his story all over again. From his own lips she heard the woeful tale of his burning love for "the false beauty," of her fickleness, and of his own wretchedness, his hopeless love. Deeply moved, she cried, "I pity you from my heart!" He looked at her, his dark eyes wide with the wonder of it, amazed at the speed with which the thoughts of Polly Woods fled from his mind. There was a kind of ecstasy in his voice as he answered her cry with a cry of his own: "Do you pity me? Then I love you for that!"

No sooner had he told her that he loved her than his health was restored to him. He declared then and there that she must marry him, but that he was going away and would not see her again until he had put by enough to "set up house upon." His ardor was so intense he did not trust himself to be near her until they should marry. For a year he worked in various engraving shops, and on an August day in 1782 he returned to her and they were married. He signed the register with his full signature; she, being unable to read or write, put her mark under his name.

They began housekeeping at 23 Green Street, Leicester Fields (now Leicester Square). Her love for him knew no limits; his for her was so intense that he was to pray (in the form of a poem called "Sexual Love") that God might pity him and keep him from destroying by the "fury" of his ardor, by his "wrath," the oneness of their union: "Pity must join together what wrath has torn in sunder." Their love was the beginning of the New Jerusalem, the New Adam and Eve, and if there was to be regeneration in the New Zion, wrath—whether the wrath of Cain or the wrath of Satan's temptation—"must be rolled up like a scroll" with the old theologies. He wrote:

I will not cease from mental fight,
  Nor shall my sword sleep in my hand,
Till we have built Jerusalem
  In England's green and pleasant land.[3]

The first few years of their marriage, like all the years of their remarkable marriage, were years of poverty. Poverty, though, had no
effect on their love and happiness. What was hindering the building of Jerusalem in England was the cruel neglect and even persecution of hopeless poor people—especially the inhumanity prac-
ticed on children and women in factories, mines, on the streets of
London by the repressive government, by the greed of the owners
of industry. As for the personal life of William and Catherine, despite poverty (or because of it) their friendship for each other knew
no flaw. They took long walks together during the day, thirty miles
at a stretch being no unusual distance. Toward evening they would
search out a wayside inn where they would dine and discuss an
endless variety of subjects. They talked openly on household matters, on poetry, on visions, on spirituality and mysticism, on imagination, and on sex. Having dined they would return home under
the light of the stars.

Often at night, when the "presences bade him" get up from bed
and write, she would get up also, sit beside him, her hand in his,
sometimes writing to his dictation. In less than one year after their
marriage, William Blake had taught his wife not only to read and
write, but to copy out his manuscripts in a hand finer than his own.
She learned to draw and to color his illuminated books. She
learned from him to see visions, his as well as her own, beholding
on one occasion a long procession of English kings and queens
"pass by with silent tread." He would read to her from Dante, from
the Bible, and from Milton. They would read *Paradise Lost,* sitting
together in the warm sun, in their small garden.

So long as William Blake had to work for others in order to earn
a living, Catherine was kept from working with him. She was able,
though, to encourage him to publish his own work, his first book of
poetry, *Poetic Sketches.* The publication of this book marked the beginning of an epoch in English literature, the opening of the long-
sealed well of Romantic poetry. The poems stand today as heralds
of the modern poetry of nature and of enthusiasm.

A year later Blake was able to give up working at engraving for others and he, with a partner, opened a printseller's shop in London. It was not a success, either financially or artistically. The shop needed financial help to survive, but no such help was forthcoming, especially not from William's family. His older brother, "Evil John," was too busy ruining the hosiery business to save the printseller's shop; James, his other brother, was very generous with "bread and cheese advice" on how to make money by mass production of prints. It was the youngest brother, Robert, who, though he could not save the shop, would appear in a vision to William and show him a method of engraving on copper that was to revolutionize the art of engraving.

Robert was the closest and dearest relative to William and Catherine, especially during the first five years of their marriage. He was very talented as an artist, a spiritually profound young boy. He worked with William in the printseller's shop as an apprentice in engraving. They were beautifully happy together, living in the same flat—until tragedy entered their lives. Robert was stricken with consumption. Day after day, night after night, William nursed his beloved brother. Neither sleeping nor so much as closing his eyes, William would not let anyone help him, not even Catherine, who, he felt, was already overburdened with keeping the household going.

William stayed with his brother until the end. Not even after he closed Robert's eyes in death, not even after the interment, did William lie down to rest. It was not until he saw his brother's spirit ascending, clapping its hands for joy, that William lay down. Then he slept without stirring for three days and three nights. Now Catherine was to watch over him, not permitting anyone to disturb his rest.

In the days and years following Robert's death William and Catherine continued to talk to him, to ask his opinion on both spiritual and worldly matters. One day he appeared to William in the spirit and taught him a better way to engrave his poems upon copper, how to print illustrations and decorative borders upon the same page with the poems. He showed William secrets of engraving that had never before been revealed to anyone on earth. The unique method revealed by Robert started William Blake on what was to prove the great works of his life. In later years he wrote to a friend of how he came into the knowledge:

> I know that our deceased friends are more really with us than when they are apparent to our mortal part. Thirteen years ago I lost a brother, and with his spirit I converse daily and hourly in the spirit, and see him in remembrance in the region of my imagination. I hear his advice, and even now write from his dictates. . . . Every mortal loss is an immortal gain. The ruins of time build mansions in eternity.[4]

The new method of engraving and of putting the poems on the same page was a catalyst to his imagination, and William Blake's work entered a period of mystical and lyrical brilliance. He gave up the printseller's shop and with Catherine once more close to him, helping him with the coloring and printing, moved into the Herculus Building in Lambeth, the southern metropolitan borough of London.

In less than six years after learning from Robert the never-before-known method of engraving, William Blake produced some of his greatest works, among them *Vala*, perhaps the most splendid and mystical of his poems; the visionary *Prophetic Books;* and the magnificent *Jerusalem.* With these there appeared from their newly purchased press prints that were written *backwards* upon the copper, written with marvelous accuracy and patience. Catherine's hand is apparent in some, her handwriting being much finer and more careful than William's. *The Songs of Innocence* was the first of the lyrics printed on their own press.

But these masterpieces brought him little recognition and even less money. He and Catherine were living on ten to fifteen shillings a week at this time. Furthermore, he was beginning to be physically exhausted. He was thirty-nine years old, and it is undoubtedly of himself he was writing when he said:

> My hands are laboured day and night,
> And ease comes never in my sight.
> My wife has no indulgence given,
> Except what comes to her from heaven.
> We eat little, we drink less;
> The earth breeds not our happiness.[5]

Added to his exhaustion was their growing apprehension that the New Jerusalem was still far away, and that "Satan in a dark cloud" was hovering over London—with evil being mistaken for good. They saw this evil everywhere they went, on the streets, in the homes, among the merchants, among the poets and artists. The songs of innocence were being drowned out by the songs of experience; the marriage of heaven and hell was not working out. On every face they saw "marks of weakness, marks of woe." Almost unbearable to them were the cries of the overworked, mistreated chimney-sweepers, the children whose emaciated bodies were the right size to fit down the dirty chimneys, the loud and angry cries of the whores, the cries of abandoned infants, the agony of wounded and dying soldiers back from the war, and the cursing of prisoners in the old Lollard's Tower (from which cursings had been heard since the year 1440). Through the fogs and miasma of London at midnight they heard but could not shut out, the "youthful harlot's curse," the curse that

> Blasts the new-born infant's tear
> And blights with plagues the marriage-hearse.[6]

William and Catherine realized that they must leave London, the beloved city that was to be their Jerusalem, the streets that were to be streets in the new Zion. After eighteen years of marriage, in the year 1800, the Blakes left London for the first time in their lives. It meant leaving their social and professional connections; it meant giving up being part of the London community of writers and artists; it meant turning their backs on the Paradise of the 1757 prophecy. Taking William's sister with them (she had been living with them after Robert's death) the three left for Felpham, a little village in Sussex some sixty or seventy English miles from London, on the English Channel.

Felpham was a beautiful place, "beloved of God and the spirits." It was the Paradise of his imagination. Here he and Catherine walked along the shore in all kinds of weather. Visions that had deserted them in London came back to them, visions in which they met all manner of kings and poets and prophets, "walking in shadowy multitudes along the edge of the sea." They were majestic shadows, gray but luminous, superior to the common height of man. Once, while writing in the garden, he saw a fairy funeral, the body being borne on a rose leaf by a procession of singing creatures the size and color of gray grasshoppers. Felpham, in contrast to Lambeth, gave to William Blake his first "vision of light" in many years. He no sooner arrived there than he wrote the poem "To Mr. Butts," expressing his happiness with Felpham:

> I stood in the streams
> Of heaven's bright beams,
> And saw Felpham sweet,
> In soft female charms . . .[7]

The poem continues, saying that once again he knew his shadow and that of his wife, his sister, and his friends:

> Away to sweet Felpham, for heaven is there,
> The ladder of angels descend through the air.

As he and Catherine stood in the village looking up to heaven, they saw the ladder, and on it Robert and their friends, "descend and ascend with bread and the wine." In another poem, meant more for Catherine than for others, he tells what his state of mind was on coming to Felpham:

> I have mental joys and mental health,
> Mental friends and mental wealth.
> I've a wife that I love and that loves me,
> I've all but riches bodily.[8]

William went to work for a Mr. William Hayley, a commercial publisher and printseller, and for a time all seemed to go well with this patron. But, before long, Hayley's worldliness, his pressuring Blake to work on prints that would sell, his callous disregard of Blake's original, mystical genius began to wear on the nerves of both William and Catherine. But the disputatious Hayley was not the sole reason for the Blakes' decision to leave Felpham; nor was it their realization that perhaps they were mistaken about Felpham being the Paradise of his imagination. There is an indication, that William's sister, who had been living with them in the same house for three years, had become an emotional and spiritual drain on

Catherine. He weighed in the balance the commands of family duty against the demands of his great love for his wife—and found his sister wanting. He wrote:

> Must the duties of life each other cross?
> Must every joy be dung and dross? . . .
> Must my wife live in my sister's bane,
> Or my sister survive on my Love's pain?[9]

His answer was a definite "No!" Three years after arriving in "sweet Felpham" (which had by now become unbearable) William and Catherine Blake returned in joy and with a sense of relief to London. What became of the sister is not known; she is not heard of again.

It was a life of poverty they returned to in London, but, except for an "interval of dark unproductiveness," it was a happy life, in which he wrote his great lyrics. Catherine—who "by unanimous consent" was considered an almost perfect wife—decorated, illuminated, and bound his books, "the most wonderful books ever made by hand." It was a thin living they earned from their hard, unremitting toil; besides this, William Blake was a poor businessman, misled and cheated by collectors. The couple lived in a flat of two rooms for seventeen years without complaining. His surroundings mattered little to William Blake, who, Catherine said, was "incessantly away in Paradise." Day in and day out, sometimes far into the night, he and Catherine labored at the creative work. He would stop only periodically to run downstairs to fetch a pot of beer from a neighboring public house. Their life together in London had become almost incredibly productive.

William Blake was barely sixty-six years old, the forty-second year of his marriage to Catherine, when the first symptoms of the gallstones that would be the cause of his death appeared. However, this did not keep him from working. He was happier than ever, in his work, his friends, and with the fact that he had become the center of a circle of young artists. In forty-five years of marriage his love for his wife had intensified, as had her love for him. They dared not think of ever being separated from each other. In 1827 he fell ill of a strange complaint, a shivering and sinking which told him he had not long to live. "I have been very near the gates of death," he said, "and have returned very weak, and an old man, feeble and tottering, but not in spirit and life, not in the real man, the imagination which liveth for ever. In that I grow stronger and stronger as the foolish body decays."

The story of William Blake's death was recorded for posterity. Catherine was present, so was a friend, and so was a "poor woman." On the day of his death, William composed songs to his maker "so sweetly to the ear of his Catherine, that when she stood to hear him, he, looking upon her most affectionately, said: 'My beloved! they are not mine! No! They are not mine.' " Seeing the joy and grief in her eyes, he took her hand in his and told her they would not be parted; he should always take care of her. Just before he died, his countenance became fair, his eyes brightened and he burst out into singing of the things he saw in Heaven—he and his Catherine in the New Jerusalem. "He made the rafters ring," and the poor woman who had come in to help Mrs. Blake cried, "The death of a saint, the death of a saint!"[10]

After his death, Catherine continued to believe him always with her in the spirit. She would call out to him at times as though he were but a few yards away. Sometimes he would talk to her. Once he told her that despite the neglect of his work, fame even on earth would be granted them. However, for her no spiritual companionship could make up for the lack of daily communion with him in the common things of life. "Are we not one-half phantoms of the earth and water?" she asked.

Catherine Blake fretted herself into the grave, surviving her husband only two years. There is no record of where she was buried.

2

Frances and Gilbert Chesterton

Gilbert Keith Chesterton, some eighty years after William Blake's death, was one of the most articulate and brilliant "discoverers" of Blake's genius. He saw in Blake's exemplary marriage the "indestructible truth" that marriage is forever. Chesterton wrote a book which is as much about himself as it is about Blake. Essential to manhood, he wrote, "is the right to bind oneself and be taken at one's word."[1] The marriage vow was almost the only vow that remained out of the whole medieval conception of chivalry; he, like Blake, was not about to give it up.

Whereas the Blakes' marriage had no relationship to any church, the Chestertons' marriage was eventually to emerge as an example of what a Catholic marriage could be at its best. Chesterton entered the Roman Catholic Church at the age of forty-eight, sixteen years after his marriage to Frances. Before his marriage to her he showed no interest in any religion and a strong aversion to Catholicism. Frances showed the same aversion to Catholicism, but felt rather strongly about her Protestantism.

Before his meeting with Frances Blogg, Gilbert Chesterton was far from an admirable person. In his youth and early manhood he had many of the bigoted traits of character we associate with the flaws of Saul of Tarsus before the meeting that turned him back from the road to Damascus. As Gilbert himself would later intimate, he was like Francis Bernardone before he met poverty and heard a voice like a bell telling him he had met his bride.

G. K. Chesterton was born in Kensington, England, of fairly well-to-do parents, on May 29, 1874. He was in some ways a very backward child, not talking much until he was three, and not learning to read until he was eight. Even in childhood, and for much of his life, his father meant more to him than his mother, which was probably due to the fact that his mother preferred the youngest son, Cecil. His father, Edward, was a liberal politically and an agnostic religiously. The family seldom went to church, and when they did, it was more for status than for prayer. Indeed, it did not matter much which church, or which denomination, they attended.

Gilbert, in his early school days, was the object of many practical jokes, which he accepted with good humor and loud laughter. He was older and bigger than his classmates, yet he chose to follow rather than to lead. Despite their tricks (like filling his pockets with snow and watching him stand in front of class dripping water), his peers respected him for his intellectual abilities and moral character—but not for his scholarship, which was less than adequate.

It is possible that Gilbert Chesterton's interest in paradoxes grew from the realization that he himself was a paradox. His intellect, even as a boy, was greatly superior to that of his fellows, but he accepted their trite opinions and prejudices instead of his own judgments. When he was eighteen, despite his own belief in justice and equality, he wallowed in the same muddy pools of hatred, bigotry, and snobbery as did his chauvinistic cronies. It was at this time that his anti-Semitism began to appear, and, typically, he was involved in a paradox. On the one hand he laughed about "the Jew" and made "the Jew" the butt of his writing, criticism, and ridicule, while on the other hand he was protesting, "Some of my best friends are Jews." (This was evidently the first time this expression was ever used.) He cited as examples of his attitude toward Jews his friendship with the brothers Lawrence and Maurice Solomon, members of the Junior Debating Club. Founded by Gilbert, the club was intended to be exclusive. However, friends or no friends, he wasn't going to let the gentile members of the club think that he, Chesterton, was a Jew-lover. At Christmas time he gave a party and invited only his close friends, writing on the invitation, "No Jews are coming." And when one of the Solomons did visit him at his home, Gilbert could not resist concluding the visit with, "Come on, I'll walk you back to the ghetto."

Chesterton was undoubtedly aware, as were his critics, that the main reason his political thinking, his socialism, and his humanism were not taken seriously was his noisy anti-Semitism. Here was one more paradox: he was anti-Semitic at the same time that he tried to convince everyone that he was not merely a witty, bigoted, anti-Semitic "journalist." While writing against "the Jew" he was also writing, "No Christian ought to be an anti-Semite, but every Christian ought to be a Zionist."[2]

Five years later Gilbert strongly supported Captain Alfred Dreyfus, the French officer accused of treason merely because he was a Jew. But no matter how much Chesterton declared his belief in equality, it seemed he protested too much. He was not believed, except by companions like Hilaire Belloc, a man of intense prejudices. Belloc became a member of the Junior Debating Club and, along with Gilbert's brother Cecil, fed the smoldering coals of Gilbert's bigotry, which at times would burst into flame.

It would be an overstatement to say that Gilbert Chesterton cast off the Old Adam and put on the New Man from the moment he met Frances Blogg. Yet what Chesterton later wrote about St. Francis of Assisi was obviously about himself too. It was also a tribute to his wife:

> He had made a fool of himself. Any man who has been young, who has ridden horses or thought himself ready for a fight, who has fancied himself as a troubadour and accepted the conventions of comradeship, will appreciate the ponderous and crushing weight of that simple phrase. The conversion of St. Francis, like the conversion of St. Paul, involved his being in some sense flung suddenly from a horse. . . . Anyhow, there was not a rag of him left that was not ridiculous. . . . He saw himself as an object, very small and distinct like a fly walking on a clear window pane; and it was unmistakably a fool. And as he stared at the word "fool" written in luminous letters before him, the word itself began to shine and change.[3]

Gilbert was not transfigured with the kind of immediacy with which we are led to believe the conversion of St. Paul and St. Francis took place. His realization of himself "as an object, very small and distinct" was much less dramatic than a blinding flash of light or falling from a horse. But it was through Frances that he became aware of the word "written in luminous letters before him."

Before he was introduced to Frances, Gilbert's comrades and intimate friends were all male; there were no women in the Junior Debating Club. No women were invited to be part of the eating, drinking, and discussing that took place in the seedy Soho restaurants around tables with stained cloths—especially at El Vino's, on Fleet Street. Along Fleet Street some irresponsible and unfounded gossip about homosexual leanings among members of the J.D.C. did not seem to have any effect on the club's attitude toward male exclusiveness. As a group it was against women's suffrage in general, and Miss Pankhurst in particular. Gilbert was writing articles which included such statements as this: "Nothing is necessary to the country except that the men should be men and the women women." He began work on his novel, *The Napoleon of Notting Hill,* a story which perhaps influenced Orwell's *1984.* The story has no female characters in it, and its dedication to Hilaire Belloc did nothing to quiet the gossip about the relationship between the two.

During this period of his life Chesterton's literary output was overwhelming. He wrote while eating, while discussing, while walking along the streets, leaning against buildings, many times writing two articles at once. But much of what he wrote at that time was shallow. He was ruining his health, not just through overwork, but through overeating, overdrinking, and continuous discussions that often lasted through the night into the early hours of morning. "They discuss just to hear their own voices," Frances was to write later.

Gilbert was beginning to get fat (his weight would ultimately reach 400 pounds) and more and more neglectful of his appearance. He had become a recognizable "character" of London. He might have been stamped for the rest of his career as a slovenly, absent-minded, brilliant, fat, "jolly journalist," thoroughly enjoying himself in "a haze of talk and uproarious laughter" in the company of the greats of the day. His acquaintances included poets, politicians, literary men, journalists, dramatists—Belloc, Shaw, Beerbohm, Baring, Barrie, Conrad, Henry James, and many others. But Frances was to change his image to that of a brilliant literary man.

Frances Blogg was a beautiful, intelligent young woman in her early twenties when Gilbert first saw her in her parent's house in Bedford Park, a garden suburb of London. He fell in love with her immediately, romantically, like a "troubadour" of medieval days. He did not tell his lady of his love for fear she would not accept him; instead, he wrote love poems to her in his notebook. There were many poets, artists, and writers (including Yeats) who lived in Bedford Park, and the Blogg household had its own club. Unlike the J.D.C., this club, the I.D.K., was made up of intellectual and brilliant persons of both sexes. (Whenever the members were asked what I.D.K. meant the answer was always, "I don't know.") Frances was the oldest of three girls. Judging by their pictures, and by the number of young men, suitors, and friends who frequented the house, the three sisters were beautiful and interesting. The father of the girls (and their young brother) had been dead for some time when Gilbert came into their lives. Once well-to-do, the family had fallen into a degree of poverty that made it necessary for the sisters to work, Frances as a secretary.

Meeting Frances was the beginning of a new life for Gilbert. Up to the time he met her he was writing in his notebook of his loneliness: "Because I have not a lady to whom to send my thought at that hour that she might crown my peace." His first entry after meeting Frances, consisted of two lines: "You are a very stupid person. I don't believe you have the least idea how nice you are."[4] Later, describing his first impression of her, he wrote, "She was a queer card. She wore a green velvet dress barred with grey fur. . . . She had an attractive face, which I should have called elvish, but that she hated all the talk about elves. . . . Physically there is not quite enough of her to carry all that temperament; she looks slight, fiery and wasted, with a face which would be a Burne Jones if it were not brave; it has the asceticism of melancholy. . . . She is fond of the Bible and very fond of dancing."[5] He described her as having the right combination of intellect and emotion, as possessing an elusive attraction, and "she wore no make-up." She attracted him spiritually and physically. There was something in her eyes that seemed to tell him how much she would mean to him in his life and in his work. In a letter he wrote about her "great heavenly eyes that seem to make the truth at the heart of things almost too terribly simple and naked for the sons of flesh."

No doubt Frances fell in love with him, if not at their first meeting, very soon after. She listened to him and he to her with a kind of truthfulness and openness neither experienced with others. He did not tell her of his love until he sensed that she might be doubting not just his sincerity, but his intelligence. When he finally overcame the fear that his peers, the comrades of Fleet Street, would censure him for betraying their togetherness, he asked Frances to marry him. She consented, but there was more censure than either anticipated. His friends reacted much as he had expected, and so did both their mothers. His mother had taken a dislike to Frances—she was too frail; she was ill; she was just "not the right wife for Gilbert." Her mother thought their marriage would be a disaster—he was too fat, ate too much, drank too much, talked a lot of socialistic nonsense, and, above all, was an "impecunious journalist." She was right about his poverty. He wrote a letter to Frances enumerating what he would bring to her if they married: about three pounds in gold and silver, a straw hat, some of his own poetry, a box of matches, a walking-stick, the letters she had written him, and a heart full of love. What her mother could not know at the time, nor did she live to find out, was that Gilbert would will to Frances a considerable fortune—property and money worth in those days over $150,000, plus future royalties and his manuscripts.

Once they were engaged, Gilbert was happy in his role of the jolly journalist, able to continue his old way of life as an engaged man without having to take on the responsibility of a married man. But if he was happy, Frances was not. She confronted him openly, and after an engagement of two years, they were married. It was what he wanted; but he did not realize it until she made clear it was what she wanted. "Frances wants it" was something he would say many times during the thirty-five years of their marriage.

They took up their life together in London. He continued to overwork, overeat, overdrink, attack "the Jew" and write little of importance. He was pushing himself to a nervous collapse, and Frances did not like what she saw. Two years after their marriage

Gilbert Keith Chesterton was being called "the fat humorist." He wore a conventional frock-coat, which he wore most unconventionally, and a silk hat over a mat of unruly hair. He was not just untidy, but a figure for ridicule. By a "stroke of genius," as Maisie Ward put it, Frances changed his appearance. Gilbert became picturesque, with a wide-brimmed slouch hat, a flowing cloak, a sword-stick, and even the butt of a pistol peeking from his pocket. (Frances was unable to get him to go to a dentist or to wear a denture, which he sorely needed.) Her image-making worked; by 1906, two years later, Gilbert Chesterton, at the age of thirty-two, had become a well-known, respected, and recognized writer, famous enough to be one of the celebrities painted and photographed for exhibitions. But beside the fact that Frances hated the life of London, and saw what harm was being done to her husband, their health was suffering because of London living. She expressed a wish to move to the country, and he, as always, wished what she wished. They moved from Battersea, London, to a small town in Buckinghamshire, Beaconsfield. They felt the inland climate would be good for her painful arthritis, and the quiet atmosphere good for his overworked heart and nervousness.

They maintained their right, as any married couple would, to live wherever they wanted. They wanted privacy, a place to care about each other. But their move to Beaconsfield stirred up a storm of protests, criticism, accusations, and vilifications against Frances. His comrades threatened to kidnap him and hide him away from the woman "who was about to ruin his journalistic career"; their parents objected, claiming they were deserting family and friends. (Yet it was Gilbert and Frances who later took care of the aged, blind mothers.) Cecil Chesterton cried out melodramatically, "She has taken my Chesterton from me!" and Belloc, in a display of his usual bad temper, shouted that now Gilbert Chesterton would be ruined as a writer, being deprived of the comradeship of the Fleet Street journalists. Frances, they said, had committed a crime against the public good by removing him to Beaconsfield. Cecil's wife, Ada, after Frances' death, wrote that Gilbert did not love Frances, but moved away from London because she "forced" him.

The truth is that the married couple were delighted with the move. At Beaconsfield Gilbert's writing reached a peak he would never have reached in London. He read his essays and poems to her, tested his ideas on her, listened to her criticisms and suggestions, depended on her encouragement, even as she listened to him and depended on his encouragement in her writings of poems, plays, and children's stories. He, of course, continued to write for the London magazines and papers, but his masterpieces, *The Everlasting Man, St. Francis of Assisi, Thomas Aquinas,* and *The Ballad Of The White Horse,* were all written during the years of their married life away from London.

They were seldom parted from each other. Even when she was too ill to travel, she went with him on his lecture tours, all over England, France, Rome, and the United States, simply because "Gilbert is so lonely without me." After ten years of marriage he still felt in her presence what he had felt when they first met; he "heard the sun and the moon and the stars singing together." It was her opinions, he said, that put him on the side of orthodox Christianity. When she was sick in the hospital after a serious operation, he suddenly understood the "mysteries of marriage" and wrote, "One of the mysteries of marriage (which must be a Sacrament and an extraordinary one) is that a man evidently useless like me can yet become at certain instants indispensable. And the further oddity is that he never feels so small as when he really knows that he is necessary."[6]

Eventually Gilbert's attitude toward Jews changed—except for the time prior to World War I when Cecil Chesterton was sued for, and found guilty of, libeling a Jew, Sir Rufus Isaacs. In his brother's defense, Gilbert wrote letters to editors attacking Jewish government officials as traitors, unpatriotic foreigners, and members of international conspiracies. However, by the time of Hitler, some Jewish leaders described Gilbert as "one of the first to speak out against Hitlerism with all the directness and frankness of a great and unabashed spirit."

Frances agonized over the plight of the Jews under Hitler and made friends with refugees. Gilbert expressed no opposition. (The year after his death, Frances, trying to piece together her shattered life, went to Germany, where she visited a university professor and his English wife, who were undergoing persecution. She was deeply moved and grieved by their suffering and peril.) Evidence of the change in Gilbert's attitude is seen in *The Everlasting Man:* "humanly speaking, the world owes God to the Jews.... They did indeed carry the fate of the world in that wooden tabernacle that held perhaps a featureless symbol and certainly an invisible god." Speaking at the Jewish West End Literary Society he said, "The Jews were a race born civilized. You never met a Jewish clod or yokel. They represented one of the highest of civilized types. . . ."

According to those who knew Gilbert and Frances personally it was obvious that "after twenty-five years of marriage, Gilbert not only loved his wife tenderly but was still ardently in love with her." By their twenty-fifth wedding anniversary he had written many poems about her and to her. In *The Ballad of the White Horse,* considered by many his greatest work, he expresses his love for his wife, his country, and his faith. The dedication to Frances says in part:

> Wherefore I bring these rhymes to you
> Who brought the cross to me,
> Since on you flaming without flaw
> I saw the sign that Guthrum saw
> When he let break his ships of awe
> And laid peace on the sea.[7]

The reference is to Guthrum, the Danish king, whose ships were destroyed at sea, who was defeated by King Alfred, and who was converted to Christianity. Likewise, Gilbert was brought to Christianity, and ultimately the Catholic church, by Frances, who "in her very being bore the meaning of peace" for him. But the poem emphasizes that all was not peace between the Danes and the English. Nor was all peace between Frances and Gilbert during their marriage. His wish was that they be accepted into the Catholic church together, but she held back, not wanting to be untrue to her Anglo-Catholic friends. At the same time she did not want to be separated from him, either physically or spiritually. The same kind of struggle went on in him. He wrote his friend Baring: "For deeper reasons than I could ever explain, my mind was to turn especially on the thought of my wife, whose life has been in many ways a very heroic tragedy, and to whom I am so much in debt of honor that I cannot bear to leave her, even psychologically, if it be possible by tact and sympathy to take her with me. We have had a very difficult time lately; but the other day she rather abruptly faced the thing herself in a new way; and spoke as if she knew where we both would end."[8] She did know. He was received into the Roman Catholic church on July 30, 1922, she four years later.

However, those four years of "separation" were a great strain on them, as was the strain illness put on them all during their marriage. There were other difficulties threatening to separate them. As far back as 1914, the strain of the war, coupled with the danger of his being sued for libel because of his violent antigovernment, anti-Semitic writings, caused Chesterton to head toward collapse. He was suffering with persistent bronchitis and indigestion. One night, returning home with Father O'Connor, Gilbert (who had been drinking heavily) stumbled in the darkness, fell and broke his arm. He then developed congestion of the larynx, and on Christmas Eve suffered a complete physical and mental collapse, his brain, stomach, and lungs affected. He remained in a coma, on and off, for four months, unconscious for some ten weeks. Frances, herself painfully ill from attacks of the chronic arthritis of the spine, was with Gilbert constantly. She was near despair. She wrote, "It is absolutely hopeless. It seems impossible to go on like this. The impossibility of reaching him is too terrible an experience and I don't know how to go through with it. I pray for strength and you must pray for me." She said it was like praying for a miracle to happen.

At Easter time, Gilbert started to recover from the coma. One day he suddenly asked for Frances, and when she sat down beside him, he hugged her. She wrote to Father O'Connor that when he hugged her she felt "like Elijah, was it? and shall go on in the strength of that hug for forty days."

Twenty years later, when their lives had been brought even closer by working together, visiting with old and new friends, sharing their religious beliefs, and caring about each other, Gilbert Chesterton again, became dangerously ill. In 1936 it became evident he was not far from dying. His breathing had become labored; he was suffering with bronchial catarrh; his conversation was slow; his mind would wander while he was dictating; then he would lapse into sleep. The doctor ordered him to bed, telling Frances a specialist was needed.

Frances herself was mortally ill, although she did not tell anyone of her suffering. After his first illness in 1914, both she and Gilbert believed his recovery was a miracle brought about by prayer; with this illness, twenty years later, Frances knew that not even prayer would help. She said, "I did not dare to pray for another miracle."

Gilbert Keith Chesterton was given Extreme Unction and received Holy Communion. He regained consciousness briefly, looked at Frances, and spoke the last six words of his life: "Hello, my darling. Hello, my dear." Then he lapsed into the coma in which he died the next morning, June 14, 1936. Ill as she was, Frances had much to do after his death and a worse suffering than her illness assailed her. She wrote to Father O'Connor: "I find it increasingly difficult to keep going. The feeling that he needs me no longer is almost unbearable. How do lovers love without each other? We were always lovers."

Barely two years later Frances Chesterton died of cancer of the spine. She had not told anyone about the cancer, so that the cause of her death was not known until later. Not even their dearest friends knew. George Bernard Shaw wrote to a friend asking, "What did Frances die of? Was it of widowhood?" Someone was heard to remark at her funeral, "She was able to suffer anything, except that separation."[9]

3

Maisie Ward and Frank Sheed

The world knew Maisie Ward and Frank Sheed as Sheed and Ward, publishers extraordinary. People thought that there was a Mr. Sheed and a Mr. Ward; Maisie wrote that it seemed almost impossible for people to grasp that she was Mrs. Sheed. "Frank complained sometimes, the nearest many people got was to say, 'How do you do, Mr. Sheed. And how is Mrs. Ward?' "[1]

Perhaps neither of them had thought seriously of marriage before meeting each other. Maisie said she had not thought about getting married at all, let alone having children, and least of all, begetting a publishing house. But suddenly one spring day, Maisie Ward and Frank Sheed were married. "A splendid honeymoon in Venice," wrote Frank. A few months later in that same year, the first offspring of their marriage was born: a publishing house.

"The foundation of Sheed and Ward was not one of the major religious happenings of 1926. That year, if my memory is right," said Frank, "saw John of the Cross made a Doctor of the Church and Thérèse of Lisieux canonized."[2] Despite the disclaimer, it was one of the major religious happenings in the first quarter of the twentieth century, for these two extraordinary people changed the whole attitude of Catholic publishing in England and the United

31

States, and perhaps in Europe. They were humanists; that is, they were religious humanists, a paradox.

The couple met at a religious fundraising. Frank Sheed was in charge of a stall called Jumble, and he sold Maisie a horrible pair of scissors, with some witticisms thrown in. She could never resist humor. At that time she was a soapbox orator in Hyde Park. "One day I was asked to take a new speaker into my squad." It was the young man from the Jumble stall. He spoke well and they needed good speakers. "I said Deo Gratias that he had come all the way from Australia to join the Catholic Evidence Guild."[3]

Maisie's father's family had long lived on the Isle of Wight, where she was born. Her grandparents were Oxford Movement converts; that is, converts from Anglicanism to Roman Catholicism—inspired by John Henry Newman, leader of the Oxford Movement. Maisie's grandfather was known as "Ideal Ward" because he wrote a book called *The Ideal of a Christian Church* after he became a Roman Catholic. Her father had entered the seminary but discovered he did not have a vocation to the priesthood. He did have a vocation as a writer of religious books, however. Both Maisie's parents were famous writers in their time; her mother was a novelist. Their friends were the famous literary and religious personages of the nineteenth century.

The Wards, absorbed in their religion and their writings, were the devoted parents of five children. But suffering came early in Maisie's life. The brother Maisie was closest to died suddenly while he was away at school. "My childhood was abruptly ended," Maisie wrote. She had always been athletic, and wanted to be a boy because "it was so much easier to climb in knickers than in a skirt."[4] Now she became inward. Her tremendous love of books saw her through the time of depression. She had an unusually gifted memory and learned quickly. Frank Sheed, writing about her after her death, said, "She had an astonishing memory—I had memorized yards of poetry myself but I had not known anyone who could quote prose at such length and with such accuracy."[5]

Such young women with intellectual gifts were called "bluestockings." They rarely could do what Maisie longed for: go up to Oxford. "The conventional thing," wrote Maisie Ward of her youth, "at that date in our world was to send your sons to a university and to present your daughters at Court and give them a London season. My parents could not afford to give a ball for us, but they did take a house in London . . . my sister and I were both presented, and we went to a good many dances."[6] But Maisie wasn't interested in dances. She studied on her own, bought French and Latin books, even read Dante in Italian and won a prize—but could not go to Oxford. Her father tried to provide her with work, and as he was editor of the *Dublin Review,* he gave her books to review.

Friends of the family tried to persuade her to be like other girls; one even tried to teach her "small talk" so she would be popular. "My dear, you really must do it! Young so-and-so says he can't ask you to dance, because last time he danced with you you asked him what he thought of Gladstone's moral character."[7]

When Maisie was with girls her age, she felt self-conscious: "I became conscious of being badly dressed and unskilled in small talk." But she really did not care to be one of the crowd, nor could she overcome her outspoken and direct temperament to attain the pretenses, the small and large hypocrisies, needed for social success. Frank Sheed writes, "You never had to ask yourself what she was getting at or what she was really thinking; she told you."[8]

The friends who came to her parents' home on weekends, like Frances and Gilbert Chesterton, appreciated her, and she preferred their company. She didn't have to worry about making small talk, keeping her weight down, or dressing elegantly.

Actually Maisie was most attractive, with a grace and a look of fine spiritedness. She was swiftly responsive to suffering, indignant over injustice, and anxious to do something about wrongs. During World War I she went to work as an aide in a small hospital run by nuns nursing wounded soldiers. She had never made a bed, but now she made twenty-five before breakfast every morning. The work was hard and the hours long, but it was not her own hardships that concerned her, but those of the nun in charge of the actual nursing. Maisie saw how exhausted she was and told the Head Surgeon, who told the Mother Superior. The Mother Superior was opposed to criticism of any sort—especially from those below her in the hierarchy, like a nurse's aide!—and fired Maisie.

"I think the last obstacle she had to conquer in herself was the difficulty of realizing that the majority of people did not react to criticism as she did—she listened to it attentively to see what truth might be in it. She spoke her mind to people, *expecting them to do the same to her.* She learnt, the hard way, that they often resented it, as if she were asserting her superiority . . . it was not in her nature to think herself superior to anybody."[9] wrote Frank Sheed.

One day Maisie's brother came into the house tremendously excited, saying, "There are Catholic speakers in the Park. One of them is magnificent." At this time, both he and Maisie were still seeking their life's work. But as soon as she heard the speaker, she knew she had found her vocation—to be a soapbox speaker in the Park! (Maisie's brother later entered the Jesuit order.)

"Our new society was called the Catholic Evidence Guild, and a New Zealander, Vernon Redwood, was the founder," Maisie wrote.[10] It was fairly revolutionary for Catholic lay persons to dare to speak on *theology,* rather than just witnessing to their conversion. And the Guild even encouraged laywomen to speak on the same platform with laymen! These pioneers of the Catholic Evidence Guild were called crackpots by some, eccentrics by others. "Our chief novelty as street speakers was that we aimed at the mind, not the emotions."

Although the word "ecumenical" did not exist for Catholics in those days, nor for the crowds who came to mock, Guild members had determined to be open, not to look down on other religions. They wanted to bring the Church into the world in a new way, but they were not sure how. Their first embarrassing discovery was their own ignorance of theology and scripture. So, from the first day they became students—in order to answer the hecklers! They took courses from top theologians to prepare for their motley crowds. Frank Sheed dated his introduction to theology "on a Tuesday evening in the spring of 1921. Maisie Ward gave us newcomers a class on the Supernatural Life. I had never heard the two words uttered together . . . I have lived in their awareness ever since."[11]

He had sprung from a family tree as remarkable as Maisie's, though very different. "Of my four grandparents, the one whose name I bear, Frank Sheed, was born in Aberdeen. He had been baptized in the Episcopal Church there, his parents had been married by the Dean: but he was a Presbyterian by the time I arrived: I doubt if he knew the difference or cared. My other three grandparents were from County Limerick, Catholics naturally."[12] As far back as Frank could remember, he and his younger brother were fought over. "Thinking as they did, our Sheed relations very properly saw it as their duty to save us from our mother's religion."[13]

Nevertheless, his mother had the children baptized; they went to Mass, learned their prayers. Their father, who was a Marxist, had not interfered. But suddenly one day he brought new suits for his two sons, told them to put them on, and took them to the Methodist Church. "I grew up on Methodism three times every Sunday, Marxism at breakfast and dinner every day, confession to Father Rohan in his study on one Saturday morning in the month, daily Mass and Communion during the two weeks of my father's annual vacation."[14] When Frank's younger brother died at the age of sixteen, he was given a Catholic funeral. This proved too much for Captain Sheed, and the whole family was "cut out of Grandpa's Will."

Like Maisie, Frank grew up with books. His mother had gone from England to Australia at the age of thirteen, spending six months on a ship, in awful hardships, including an outbreak of cholera. She was a child of the Irish Maloneys, farmers in County Limerick, who had been reduced to destitution by the Great Famine. Her faith and her love of scholars and scholarship brought her through. It was from her that Frank received his passion for books. She loved to read the classics, and introduced him when he was nine years old to the novels of Dickens and Scott. Later in life she would tell Maisie that she had to read to escape from the "small talk" of the ladies of her time.

Although there was not much money, Frank received a good education because of his outstanding intelligence and his habit of reading. "Approaching seventeen I was able to enter the university as one of a couple of hundred holders of bursaries or exhibitions."[15] In those years, though he was an ardent Catholic, he did not dream of learning about the Church. "I never opened a theological or spiritual book and never felt the slightest desire to."[16]

He was studying for his law degree at Sydney University Law School, a four-year course, when—at the end of his second year—he decided to take a year off and go to Europe. "When the ship arrived in England I saw my future clearly. I would enjoy my year in Europe, I would go back to Sydney and practice law."[17] He had no intention of staying in London. Then he met Maisie. "She was like the freshest wind that ever blew." He decided to stay a while and looked for a job. He got one as organizing secretary for the Catholic Truth Society. He was sure it would be just for a year; then he would go back to Sydney and finish his law studies.

The first time he spoke on the platform with Maisie was burned into his memory. "It was at Finsbury Park. The senior speaker, a woman, had a vast crowd. She came down. I got up. In five minutes I had lost them all. She got me down, got up herself, and won the crowd back. I touched a low point in misery. I was able to balance things up later by marrying her: but the wound still throbs faintly."[18]

Their lectures usually took fifteen minutes; the rest of the time the crowd questioned them and heckled. They had to be a jump ahead, and went feverishly to their study courses. "We talked theology with one another all the time—at the meal we ate together before the class, on our way to and from the outdoor meetings . . . ."[19]

Instead of one year, Frank remained in London for four. "In those four years I read practically nothing that had not a bearing on the Faith. I lived, breathed, ate, slept, theology. Yes, I slept it." Even his dreams were theological. In one dream he saw "quite clearly how man's freedom could be reconciled with God's eternal foreknowledge"[20]—the only trouble was he forgot the answer. Frank and Maisie shared the strange ecstasy, the highs of their work in the Catholic Evidence Guild, and they shared the lows. Hecklers threw ripe tomatoes; they paid pennies to children to run pins into the ankles of the speakers; drunks shook the platform, once so violently the speaker was thrown off. Then there was the woman who prayed loudly for Frank during the whole meeting.

Both of them gave themselves utterly to every crowd, large or small. They saw the work on the "soapbox" (an outdoor platform, but just as shaky as a soapbox) as "a small part of the Church's effort to get loose from the civilization that is passing away and to insert herself as a living ferment into that new civilization which is in danger of being swallowed up by paganism." They were invited to talk together to various groups, and would go up on the night train to Birmingham or Liverpool or Manchester, and the more time they spent together the more time they wanted to spend together. Frank began defending eloquently the rights of women to take important leadership roles in Catholic preaching and teaching. One pair of speakers, against women in leadership roles, had married, and the wife stopped her platform speaking, saying only husbands should speak, and if Guild members married, it was the wife's duty to stop speaking. They declared that since she had stopped speaking, Maisie must do the same the moment she and Frank married. When Frank asked the husband why his wife had to stop speaking the instant she got married, he replied, "I can't imagine Our Lady on an outdoor platform." Frank remarked dryly, "I can't imagine Our Lady married to you."

When he proposed to Maisie, Frank decided that to be ready for family life he must return to law school and get his degree, so as to be a man of substance. "On the Feast of the Assumption in 1924, I asked Maisie Ward to marry me. I returned to Sydney to finish my law course . . . after four years."[21] The Dean agreed to let him do the last two years in one. This meant attending a double set of lectures while also teaching at St. Aloysius College two hours every morning to support himself. He also taught a Workers' Group at night and every Sunday afternoon got on a soapbox under a tree and addressed whoever would listen.

"The street corner work was in my blood." Soon this new branch of the Catholic Evidence Guild drew other Catholics who wanted to speak, so Frank conducted a training class for speakers one night a week.

When Frank proposed to her, Maisie said she needed time to think it over. "Why I needed to think it over the Lord alone knows." She was writing to him every day, but perhaps she had to get over the habit of thinking she would never marry. Maisie was not against marriage, but all her experiences as a "debutante"—being presented at Court, the London season, going to the dances—had impressed her with the awareness that she did not fit into that kind of traditional mating game. She was too independent intellectually and spiritually—as were many girls of her class. In truth, it was the young women of the English gentry, the aristocracy, who were the leaders of the feminists.

As soon as Frank arrived in Australia, Maisie's telegram came accepting him. Now he worked at an even more furious pace. "I remember my law finals: sixteen three-hour papers in two scorching hot weeks. The last was on a Friday. On Saturday I staggered on to the ship for England. At Marseilles I received a telegram that I had passed. And that was the end of my legal career."[22]

Maisie had to get everything ready for the wedding by herself. Her engagement ring even came by mail. "It was a curious feeling being engaged all by myself, getting everything ready."

But at last the bridegroom arrived safely, the day came, and they were married "from Egypt House, my brother giving me away." One of her aunts gave them a gift of silver, with the admonition to have Frank's crest put on the spoons and forks at her expense. Maisie wondered if the crest should be a Koala bear or a kangaroo. She wasn't worried about her relatives meeting Frank; she was worried about Frank having to meet them. "Frank had to undergo the experience of meeting all of them at once."[23]

This experience could be perilous—she knew, because she herself was not very calm when she discovered some of her relatives in a crowd she was addressing. One aunt told her "with a smile that a hat I was wearing looked just like a Salvation Army Lassie's bonnet." (It is easy to see Maisie in the part of George Bernard Shaw's *Major Barbara*. She had style.)

The Guild members' great drawing power stemmed from both their open attitude and the dramatic way they made their points. One of the most brilliant of their soapbox speakers, Father Vincent McNabb, would do strange and dramatic things—one time kneeling in Parliament Hill Fields to kiss the feet of a particularly nasty heckler. Crowds came to hear them, for they never knew what was in store.

It was Maisie's mother who conceived the idea of a publishing house. Worried about the future of the young couple, and not wanting Maisie to go off to Australia, or some other faraway place, she suggested they start a Catholic publishing house right where they were. She had always dreamed of a good Catholic publishing house, for it was difficult for Catholic writers to find Catholic publishers of good books. There were Catholic publishers, but they published prayer books, "or else, like Herders, immense books for the specialist." Maisie's mother and father had been published by Longmans, but her mother convinced them that it would be an enormous benefit to the intelligent Catholic reading public if a Catholic publishing house brought out quality books, not works of piety, but a literature, a body of distinguished writing "with a mind," the Catholic mind at its finest.

"No one could have been more 'euphorious' than my wife and I. . . . We did not for a while realize how small was the Catholic reading public for books just above the middle of the brow. That we had to learn, painfully" wrote Frank.[24] They learned together, for neither they nor their many writer friends knew a thing about publishing. They had no problem getting great Catholic writers. Chesterton, though under contract for thirty books with various publishers, gave them a book of poems for a wedding present, and later, many of his major writings. Another wedding present came from Father Martindale, the famous priest writer; Hilaire Belloc offered them *A Companion to Wells' Outline of History.* "There we sat in 31 Paternoster Row without telephone or electricity . . . every day we received from Mr. Belloc lengthy letters of advice on publishing—looking back I should say that he knew, if possible, less than we did."[25]

Their capital was small. The great Depression was beginning just as the twenties were ending and the thirties being born. Every other Catholic publisher sold statues, rosaries, breviaries, missals. They alone declared, "We do not sell crucifixes, statues, rosary beads or medals; we sell books."

To present "the full Catholic mind" was their vision. It meant that they were going counter to the popular mentality. Their books would appeal "only to people accustomed to mental effort in their reading." Frank Sheed wrote, "All who run can *not* read this sort of book. They must be prepared to settle down to it, really to work." They wondered if they could actually sell books demanding mental effort, and they also wondered "would Catholics accept a true picture of themselves, not tricked out for the photographer—in history, biography, lives of saints and comment on contemporary events?"[26] There was yet another question: would non-Catholics respond "to the truth in Catholicism thus seriously and non-controversially presented"? Almost immediately their books were banned in Ireland. For those times, they were making a revolution!

The intellectuals were entranced. Within two years Sheed and Ward had on their list the greatest thinkers of the era. Christopher Dawson, a profound historian and philosophic spirit (who with

Edward Watkin, another philosopher, both converts from Angli-can background, were changing the very look of modern religious understanding) brought them his book *Progress and Religion.* It was the book that would inspire thinkers for decades, for in it he set forth the seminal idea that all cultures must grow from the root of religion. Christian culture courses, inspired by Dawson, were set up in universities. And it was Sheed and Ward who were making these tremendous expansions of religious mentality and spirituality pos-sible. Soon they were known as the publishers of the best in Catho-lic letters. Their lists appear, to this day, unparalleled: Karl Adam's *Spirit of Catholicism,* Père de Lubac's *Drama of Atheist Hu-manism,* Sigrid Undset's *Catherine of Siena,* the works of Newman, Mauriac, Caryll Houselander, Berdyaev, and many others who in-fluenced generations to come, appeared with Sheed and Ward.

In the midst of all this, Maisie became pregnant. In those days there was little preparation for childbearing. She was not put on a diet. "Already fat, I became enormous." She was taught no special exercises, but being naturally energetic, she did what she always did. One day, swinging herself nimbly onto a bus, she nearly had a miscarriage. From then on she was cautious. She gave birth to a healthy little girl, but afterwards she was very ill. She had a blood-clot on her lung that burst, and other clots formed in her arms and legs. For weeks she was near death.

Frank would not go to work. "He seemed to be always at hand ... went little to the office. I remember in a good evening hour his reading Dickens to me." He sang to her; he enjoyed singing. There was one song during this illness she loved, and she asked him to sing it over and over. "He who would valiant be / 'Gainst all disas-ter / Let him with constancy / Follow the Master."[27] The words were from Bunyan's *Pilgrim's Progress.*

The doctor said only surgery could save her life, collapsing the lung then artificially inflating it every six weeks. "I should have been more or less an invalid." On the eve of the surgery, the Guild members said special prayers at a famous shrine, at Tyburn. When the surgeon arrived, he decided at the last minute to "give nature one more chance." When Maisie fell asleep that night, she slept dreamlessly without drugs and awoke in the morning hungry. She got well. She was sure that although "God works through nature and through doctors," in her case, God had worked through prayer. "That this cure of mine was a special cure in answer to prayer I shall never doubt."[28]

Frank and Maisie decided to find a house so they could have a large family. They found the house, but Maisie had a tendency to miscarry and "only succeeded in producing one more—Wilfrid John Joseph." But it was a big enough family, considering that they were constantly adopting people. Frank's mother had come from Australia, and though at first Maisie had been warned about problems with mothers moving in, she soon found her mother-in-law was a liberating spirit. She wanted Frank and Maisie to be free to go and to do! "Frank and I were happy to realize that we could go away together, that Grandmother would give the children the care that only love can give, combined with complete loyalty to us."[29]

The house they had found was in the country, with buildings and land. They turned the stable into a chapel in thanksgiving for Maisie's cure, and soon people discovered it—"there were more than the small chapel could hold and Catholics wanting to join . . . plus Catholic families moving into the neighborhood." Two lively children, grandmothers, many cousins, uncles and aunts, plus a publishing house with many writers on their lists as personal friends, and the many readers who wrote also, plus the priests for the chapel, and all the others who were starting new religious movements, made a very large family. But Maisie—ahead of her time—thought of an even larger "extended family."

A Scottish Catholic Land Association was taking boys out of the slums and training them on farms. Maisie thought they should take a group. After all they had the land. "My unfortunate husband had only moved even to Horley on condition that I would not ask him to garden—and here he was involved in a mysterious farm from which I proposed to wring our daily bread, as instructed by the Distributist League and the Scottish Land Association."[30] But Frank was right; farming turned out to require much more skill than either Maisie or the Scottish Catholic Land Association had imagined. Maisie's mother said they needed a rest—a change.

With immense relief they accepted an invitation to lecture in the United States, and soon had left the farm and its complications behind them. They arrived in the United States almost simultaneously with the Wall Street crash in 1929, but this did not dampen the occasion. They were received enthusiastically and more invitations were pressed on them. As they had no idea of distances in the United States, they accepted almost everything, and then discovered that they had to travel, sometimes without a break, from one place to another.

Though exhausting, it was exhilarating, a new experience. They were popular! Everyone seemed to want them to start a branch of their publishing house in the United States without delay. But they had no such thought. Now that they had had their change, they were anxious to get back to their children and their writers, and to their own writings. But the American connection had been established. Henceforth life became a kind of juggling act, trying to keep everything going—home, children, publishing house, Catholic Evidence Guild, plus all the other religious movements they got into. Thanks to the two grandmothers, they were able to keep all their activities from crashing around them until Maisie's mother suddenly died while they were in the United States. When Maisie got the news, she and Frank were lecturing in different places. She had trouble reaching him and had to make the sad journey home alone, experiencing the pangs of regret at not being there when her mother died.

The following winter Maisie stayed home, while Frank went back to New York alone to open the New York office of Sheed and Ward. "A time was beginning for both of us of tremendous energies and considerable strain. Frank was now going to the United States three times a year . . . ."

Keeping their own little personal family life in balance was not easy. They moved back to London, but the children had no place to play, and people in adjoining houses disapproved of two lively, noisy children. Just then the tenants in their house in the country left, so they moved back. It was perfect. They determined to keep Chestnuts (as they had named their home when they bought it) always. It would be their sanctuary. But their lives and times were to unfold in greater and greater complications, and stability of the home was to become, finally, an impossible dream. Their stability would have to be in themselves.

On one of their lecture tours Frank and Maisie met Peter Maurin and Dorothy Day and immediately adopted the Catholic Worker movement. Maisie later wrote that they were "Third

Order Catholic Workers." They were to be "Third Order Friendship House Friends," too, as soon as they met Catherine De Hueck, the Baroness, later Catherine Doherty. They published her books and assisted her foundations also.

The Sheed and Ward community was a special phenomenon, developing out of Maisie and Frank and their adventuresome marriage. For great numbers of people of religious or spiritual bent, this family publishing house was their school of idealism, humanism, and religious continuity. Maisie and Frank felt that they, too, were learning. Frank wrote, "My concern with that curious firm lies in the part publishing played in my maturing as a Catholic. The books we published had their influence on vast numbers of Catholics; but on no one more than me. I see myself very much as one of Sheed and Ward's public."[31]

One September day in 1939 Maisie was in the chapel. Frank, who "was listening to the radio, came in and whispered that war had been declared." An old world was ending.

Children were evacuated from London, "their boxed gas masks hanging around their necks." Maisie and Frank offered their country home, and daughter Rosemary, aged twelve, conducted classes for the little ones. But the children were disturbed, mischievous and difficult. Maisie went back to one of her favorite dreams, a communal farm. "You would think I had had enough of trying to grow food—but in fact this was my main preoccupation in the first weeks."

It was the period of the "phoney war." Those who had evacuated their children decided to take them back; it was too lonely. There was that strange lull before the storm, a lull that at first seemed hopeful. On the farm all was steady, under control, so Maisie and Frank decided they could take a normal business and lecture tour in the States. They returned home just in time for the Battle of Dunkirk—"the small British army, almost encircled, was brought back by hundreds of civilians whose trade or hobby was the handling of a boat."

The storm broke. Friends begged Frank and Maisie to send the children over to the States. A committee from a boys' orphanage implored them to "let Chestnuts to them so that they could move their boys to safety." They faced the problem of a split existence. "Neither the London nor the New York office could be left to itself;

Frank must go to and fro." And what if bombs fell while they were away, or separated (as they had been when Dunkirk came) from their children and Grandmother? "We would either all go down together . . . or else establish Grandmother and the children in the States and ourselves go back and forth between London and New York."

In the United States they were welcomed by friends with a large house in Philadelphia, a lovely garden, even a Polish priest to teach them bee-keeping. But the children were unhappy, especially Wilfrid. And Frank was the only one who could get a permit to go back and forth to England when necessary. Separation became a way of life. He was in England when the bombs fell. "On the night of 30 December 1940 came the near-annihilation of the printed word in England, in which we and so many publishers were involved," wrote Frank. Everyone had gone from that part of London for the weekend. On Monday morning, when Frank returned, "there was just a handful of bricks in a hole. The big incendiary raid of the night before had wiped out most of Paternoster Row. Of our place nothing at all survived—all our books were destroyed and all our records. . . ."[32]

Personal tragedies became everyday occurrences. Maisie's Jesuit priest brother, Leo, for long a missionary in Japan, was interned after Pearl Harbor; later he was told to leave Japan. On the way home he became fatally ill with encephalitis and was buried at sea.

But more illness was to visit the family. On a vacation with daughter Rosemary in Canada, Maisie came down with pneumonia. Upon her recovery, she received a phone call saying that Wilfrid, aged thirteen, had contracted polio. They tried to get back quickly, but though the war was nearly over there was still no quick movement for civilians. "It seemed an eternity of waiting"—but at last they were with Wilfrid.

After they brought him home and he began to recover, Maisie discovered something about herself—she was just like all mothers: "I have always tended to be a fusser; when any of my family are late I invariably imagine some frightful accident. One night I got a lesson. Wilfrid had gone out with a friend, and at past midnight I felt I *must* check; he might be at his friend's home or both boys might still be out together, but *if* his friend had long been home?—

What happened was that I woke up both the parents, whose reaction was anger with their son. That was the last time I did any checking."[33]

In France, a new generation of young seminarians were abandoning traditional schooling to enter the priest-worker movement, training for six months in a factory or on a farm. Maisie and Frank were drawn to their cause and took off for France. "Some Capuchins had put up a wooden shack . . . they worked in a factory and made their poor place a free lodging for any homeless person."[34] They discovered Abbé Pierre, who was also providing shelter for the many homeless, and soon adopted him too, asking for his writings and telling his story.

Homelessness was particularly significant in the spirituality of Frank and Maisie. They understood it, and they saw that marriage was threatened when there was no home for a family. Maisie had started a Housing Aid Society when the Second World War left families homeless. The idea was to fund families who had lost their homes in the bombings of World War II so they could make a payment on another house. Now she and Frank got into a housing movement in upstate New York.

Then Frank's mother fell, and from that time she began to fail. The nurse woke them one night, saying the end was near, and the whole family—Frank and Maisie and Wilfrid and Rosemary were by her side. "Her beauty after death was quite extraordinary."

Both grandmothers were gone, and they themselves were now the grandparents. It did not seem possible that the soapbox lovers had been married for half a century. They wrote about life in a marriage that included such a huge family—not just their own private family, but their whole Church—everyone in it and everyone outside of it, the crowds around the soap boxes, and the hecklers.

They had lived with criticism their whole married life—criticism from relatives, criticism from hecklers, criticism from the clergy, criticism from censors, criticism from nuns, criticism from readers. And sometimes they pondered the way people turned away from The Word—especially the words in books of spirit and thought. Frank wrote:

Catholic America was fascinated by the Catholic Intellectual Revival . . . I was always being asked to lecture on the subject . . . at least twenty times a year. But not only did it not produce writers as it had in England: it did not produce any great number of readers. If only the people who thronged to hear about the surge of new Catholic writers had been willing to read them, we should have nothing left for avarice to dream about. But limitless as the interest in the writers was, it did not extend to their actual writings.[35]

Sometimes Maisie felt tears of hot rage surge up at all the criticisms. It was hard to be "different," and both of them had to school themselves to accept the fact that "the Catholic who is different and therefore difficult is felt to be a nuisance." Yet they could not and would not, ever swerve from the ideals and the religious passion that infused their union.

There were other tears, tears too deep for shedding. Rosemary and her husband, Neil Middleton, lost their first child—the first grandchild. "We buried the child of nine weeks beside his great-grandmother of eighty-five years. She surely was waiting to bid him welcome with my own mother and father and my two brothers. . . ."

One morning a letter arrived for Frank from the Archbishop's House. He opened it, expecting to be in hot water again for some rash publication. To their amazement he read aloud that Rome was making him a Doctor of Theology. So after all the years of criticism and resentment that a lay person should presume to speak of theology, the accolade had come.

The nearest he had ever been to such acceptance of his theological talks had been once in Boston, when the chairman introduced him to the audience: "The next time I introduce our speaker, I hope it will be as Frank Cardinal Sheed." That time he had responded, "Frank Cardinal Sheed will never appear on this platform without Maisie Cardinal Ward."[36] He had never wished to be vested with any ecclesiastical authority and had always said of himself that he was simply "a husband and father, a businessman given to the study of theology."

On a cold Sunday in Hyde Park, Frank fell off the speaker's stand and suffered a severe concussion. He had been "overworking furiously," and now he realized that he had to slow down. He got well slowly, but some things were never cured, like the buzzing in his ear.

Frank and Maisie had been told a lot about serene old age, but serene old age was not for them. They were in the midst of a new exercise in learning, even more new and radical than the learning they had to undertake when they first got up on soapboxes for the Catholic Evidence Guild. For suddenly the Church was changing—Vatican II and Pope John XXIII had arrived.

Everything suddenly coalesced. All the spiritually fertilizing works of the forerunners, Newman, Teilhard de Chardin, Maritain, Dawson—so many of them made accessible to the public through the publishing house of Sheed and Ward—flowered in a confusion of blooms! But the one clarification necessary appeared in the midst of the confusion; Pope John XXIII summarized it, essentially, as the blossoming of a truly Catholic mind. Catholic spirituality clearly was not a cult to be ritually observed in isolation from the world and the human condition in that world.

Certain persons are called to go beyond their own self-realization. Certain marriages are called to go beyond their own self-fulfillment. Such was the marriage of Sheed and Ward; yet self-fulfillment was also to be given them, in a union which was long and exciting to the very last.

Maisie died when she was eighty-one. In that last year of their life together she insisted that Frank must keep an appointment he had made to go to Paray-le-Monial to read a paper. He wished to cancel the journey, but she would not let him do it. He went, and returned in time to be with her for the last months. Later he wrote a book based on the Paray-le-Monial paper, on the revelations of the Sacred Heart to Saint Margaret Mary Alacoque.

> It was in effect a study of Scripture's use of "heart" as the organ not only of love but of all our willed activities, hate included. It is intellect and will fused into one principle of action, an instructed heart. . . . my mind was forced back to the time of its writing and her dying. Gradually I came to feel that a study of one individual heart—and hers was the one I had observed closest—might make a useful introduction to a more general study of the human heart in its relation to God and man. And it would enable me to discharge some of my immeasurable debt to her. . . .[37]

The year before Maisie died she had written in her last book that she felt the same immeasurable debt to him: "There is a profound joy in the fulfilment of married love."

On November 20, 1981, Frank Sheed died. He was eighty-four.

4

Olivia and Samuel Clemens

"Some people when married gain each other. Some only lose themselves," said Chesterton in a lecture given in 1905. Samuel Clemens, who at the time had been married for thirty-five years and was just five years away from the end of his life, would have agreed with Chesterton's epigram about marriage, even though it is most improbable he heard or read the speech. Both the Englishman and the American were criticized without mercy for allowing themselves to be "changed" by their marriages. Chesterton's critics wanted him to be the "Jolly Journalist"; Mark Twain's critics wanted him to remain the "foremost American humorist," damning the whole human race. Critics expressed no sympathy when personal tragedy brought agony to the lives and marriages of their witty and brilliant entertainers. "Bless your heart, they don't mind, they're exceedingly kind; they don't mind just so long as you're funny," wrote W. S. Gilbert in the operetta *The Yeoman of the Guard.*

In June of 1867 Samuel Langhorne Clemens, already known as Mark Twain, was given a commission to contribute travel letters to the San Francisco newspaper *Alta California.* He joined a party on the steamship *Quaker City* for a world tour. It was on board this paddle-wheel steamer that he fell in love with a picture, an ivory miniature of a girl, Olivia Langdon. He fell so deeply in love he never came to the surface again.

Many of the "pilgrims" aboard the steamer were hardly the kind of people Clemens would be drawn to. Furthermore, while aboard, he was "Mark Twain, Actor," playing the part of an entertainer, journalist, practical joker, a somewhat cynical, funny *raconteur* and *bon vivant.* The Congregationalist pilgrims' chief amusements were "prayers, dominoes, and backbiting." Mark Twain's chief interest on the trip was to get the travel letters written on time for the newspaper's deadline. His other interests consisted of being admired and lionized, telling stories, and singing songs. The songs he sang, to the great joy of captain, crew, and admirers, were a shade more "proper" than the songs he once sang—like "The Doleful Ballad of the Rejected Lover," which he used to warble with his pal Steve Gillis as they roamed the night streets of San Francisco. Even so, of one song he sang on board the streamer he later wrote, "It wasn't a nice song—for a parlor, anyway."

Such was the role that entertainer Mark Twain played in the early part of the pilgrimage to the Holy Land. Then, on a specific day in September—a day that to the end of his life he would hold as the beginning of his "greatest rapture"—while the *Quaker City* was in the Bay of Smyrna, he lost interest in the role he had been playing. Aged thirty-four, a self-proclaimed virgin (and proud of it), he switched roles: from Mark Twain, *bon vivant,* to Samuel Clemens, passionate lover and champion of monogamy. He fell in love with a face on a tinted ivory miniature, the face of a girl he had never met.

On that "fateful September day" the popular Mark Twain was asked to read his travel letters. Among the group gathered to hear him read was a boy of eighteen, Charles Jervis Langdon of Elmira, New York, who had conceived a deep admiration for the popular entertainer. With some trepidation about being refused by the great man, Charles Langdon invited Mr. Clemens to his cabin, and, boy-like, exhibited his treasures. He showed him the ivory miniature of his sister Olivia. Clemens looked at it "with long admiration, and spoke of it reverently." Time and time again he returned to the boy's cabin and asked to see the picture. He resolved then and there that some day he would meet the owner of that face. As was his lifelong habit, Mark Twain sang every morning before breakfast; only from then on, for the rest of the cruise, he sang no more bawdy songs—he sang spirituals.

When the cruise was finished, Samuel Clemens went to New York to spend Christmas with friends, a sort of reunion of his acquaintances made during the Mediterranean tour. Charles Langdon's family was spending Christmas in New York, staying at the St. Nicholas Hotel on Broadway. Young Langdon was anxious for them to meet the famous humorist, and two days before Christmas Mr. Clemens was invited to dine with them at the hotel. He, of course, accepted with joy; the lovely face on the tinted miniature had often been part of his waking dreams since the cruise, and now for the first time he looked upon the picture's reality. Facing him in the parlors of the St. Nicholas was the wealthy coal-dealer's only daughter, Olivia, a slender figure, pale and lovely, with great sweetness and dignity, her azure eyes peering with a tender myopic vagueness, her black tresses combed severely back from a high white forehead. Long afterwards he wrote, "It is forty years ago. From that day to this she has never been out of my mind."

Olivia Langdon was twenty-two at that first meeting. Though no longer in the shattered health of her girlhood, she was still not robust. When she was sixteen she had fallen on the ice and became a complete invalid, confined to her bed for two years. Her recovery had been gradual. During the first dinner together with her family, Clemens hinted at visiting Olivia in Elmira, and was invited to spend a week at the Langdons' millionaire estate. On the day he was to leave for the visit, Clemens, as was characteristic of him, took the slow train by mistake, rather than the fast one he was instructed to take. Not wishing to cause the family worry or trouble, he telegraphed his approach from different station stops along the way, finally arriving at the one where young Langdon was waiting. The boy was chagrined at seeing his guest in a yellow, travel-stained duster and battered straw hat looking shabby and hopelessly out of style.

Charles Langdon greeted him warmly, but unable to keep his doubts to himself, he asked, as they traveled toward Elmira, "You've got some other clothes, haven't you, Mr. Clemens?"

"Oh yes. I've got a fine brand-new outfit in this bag, all but a hat, which I'll buy. You won't know me in the morning."

Clemens did buy a hat, but even so, Charles sneaked his guest in through a back door. However, when Samuel appeared in the morning, correctly, even elegantly dressed, he was immediately accepted, and an enjoyable week of visiting followed. During this week he concluded he could not live without Olivia—Livy, as they called her, that in his heart "there was room for only one woman in all the world." Clemens had an old-fashioned Southern respect for courtship conventions, which dictated that the last day of a visit must be the last day, without exception! He agonized when the last day came, hoping they would ask him to stay longer. But nobody did. Desperately, he took Charles aside and said, "Charley, I'm in love with your sister and am going to marry her."

Charles was horrified. Much as he respected the famous Mark Twain, the thought of his wanting to take away his sister, whom he regarded as little short of a saint, made him wish he had never met this humorist. "Look here, Clemens," he said, "there's a train out of here in a half an hour. I'll help you catch it. Don't wait till tonight. Go now!"

In his deliberate way of speaking, Clemens answered, "No, Charley, I want to enjoy your hospitality a little longer. I promise to be circumspect and I'll go tonight."

That night he and Charles climbed into a light, two-seated wagon, the coachman in front, they on the back seat. As the wagon started out, the horses sprang forward, the back seat loosened, seat and passengers were catapulted through space and came down with force on the cobbled street. Neither was seriously hurt, Clemens, only dazed. When the Langdon household gathered around with restoratives, he saw to it that he did not recover too quickly from an unconscious condition. It was "the best portrayal of being knocked unconscious I've seen on any stage," he later admitted. He allowed them to support him into the house, place him in an armchair, and apply remedies. Olivia especially showed anxiety and attention, which was pure happiness to the man who had come to visit for one week only.

Two weeks later Samuel was still there, and would have remained even longer were it not that he had a speaking engagement in Cleveland, Ohio. The family was reluctant to see him leave, and so were the servants.

After the Cleveland lecture, he returned to Elmira, having made known his wish to court Olivia. She, having received letters from him every day, had by this time fallen as passionately in love with him as he with her. "They had tested each other's existence with a kiss." Jervis Langdon had his doubts, and withheld his consent to a formal engagement until he could investigate the suitor's "Western past." He asked Clemens for names of those in his past who would recommend him and sent out letters of inquiry. It was not until January that some answers came, and Mark returned with some misgivings to the Langdon home to learn his fate. He asked, "You've heard from the gentlemen out there?"

"Yes."

"They don't appear to have been very enthusiastic, from your manner?"

"Well, yes. Some of them were. . . . They agree unanimously that you are a brilliant, able man, a man with a future, and that you would make the worst husband on record." Mr. Langdon asked Clemens if he had anyone else in mind who might speak for him.

"None whose testimony would be valuable, apparently."

Jervis Langdon held out his hand: "You have at least one. I believe in you better than they do."[1]

And so the engagement of Samuel Langhorne Clemens, aged thirty-four, and Olivia Lewis Langdon, aged twenty-three, took place on February 4, 1869. No date was set for the marriage. Samuel had to fulfill lecture dates and left Elmira. He wrote to his mother, "It may be a good while before we are married, for I am not rich enough to give her a comfortable home right away, and I don't want anybody's help." Mrs. Langdon, suspicious about Mr. Clemens' motives for wanting to marry her Livy, expressed regrets for having given her consent to the engagement. When Clemens heard this he wrote to her that he did not wish to marry Miss Langdon for her wealth, as Miss Langdon knew perfectly well. As far as he and Miss Langdon were concerned, continued Clemens, Mr. Langdon could cut her off without a cent. And to Livy, who expressed a fear that she would not ever be a robust wife, he poured out his feelings: "I believe in you, even as I believe in the Savior in whose hands our destinies are. I have faith in you. I do love, love, love you, Livy!"

From the day of their engagement to the end of their lives, Samuel and Olivia were never separated from each other. When not physically in each other's presence (when he was away lecturing, mostly) they kept in close touch with one another, writing letters every day and many times twice a day. Their love letters, not made public until some forty years after Mark Twain's death, when they were released for publication by his daughter Clara, tell more than any conjectures of their dependence on each other. From the first days of his engagement he could not keep from thinking of her, of the wonder, the mystery, the strangeness of it—that there should be only one woman among the hundreds of thousands in the world whom he could love with his whole heart—that it should be his amazing good fortune to secure that one woman's love.

There have been biographers and critics (particularly Van Wyck Brooks and Stephen Leacock) who have set out to "destroy the myth of Olivia Clemens as the perfect wife for Mark Twain." They claimed she destroyed him as a cynical humorist, a writer of *galgenhumor* (gallows humor), that she turned him from Mark Twain, entertainer, into Mr. Samuel Clemens, writer of literature. "She not only edited his writing, she edited him," Brooks complained. But not all critics have read the love letters, and could not know that he felt himself an insignificant entertainer-humorist before he met Olivia Langdon. They could not know that he stated over and over that he depended completely, willingly on her judgment, her taste, her sensitivity, her religious and moral discernment. And it was what he wanted.

Samuel and Olivia were married in the Langdon's Elmira home on a beautiful June day in 1870. There were some who said openly that two such people of different backgrounds should not marry. They said that Olivia was in complete contrast to her dynamic lover. She was as delicate as he was robust, as devout as he was sceptical, as orthodox as he was unconventional. He was, according to his own evaluation, undemonstrative. He said that his entire family was undemonstrative, that he never saw his parents kiss each other, their marriage a loveless union. He contrasted his reluctance for showing his feeling with her ardor: "She poured out her prodigal affections in kisses and caresses, and in a vocabulary of endearments, whose profusion was always an astonishment to me." From the beginning he and Olivia fell deeply and physically in love with each other, a love that grew more deep as the years took their toll. "Love seems the swiftest, but it is the slowest of all growths. No man or woman really knows what perfect love is until they have been married a quarter of a century," he wrote twenty-five years later.

As a wedding gift his millionaire father-in-law gave them a completely paid for, completely furnished (including a cook, a house-maid, and a coachman) beautiful house in Buffalo, New York. He wrote to Jervis Langdon, thanking him for the lavish gift that had made Livy especially happy:

> I wasted thirty years of life, since I should have married her in early infancy, instead of wasting time cutting teeth and breaking crockery. . . . We sit alone in the loveliest of libraries, in the evening, and I read poetry—and every now and then I look up to her for loving sympathy and she inquires whether they sell sirloin steaks by the pound or by the yard.[2]

Olivia, leaning over him as he wrote, took the pen from his hand and added to his letter: "Youth is a wicked tease and I love him." ("Youth" was the name she would always use for her husband.)

The most creative years of Mark Twain, the writer, and Samuel Clemens, the man, began with his marriage to Olivia. She believed in him as a great American man of letters, and refused to allow him to make of himself a cynical satirist damning the whole human race. She knew better, knew of his great compassion for the poor, the oppressed, the downtrodden, and his unswerving concern for struggling artists, for all rebels against tyranny. He submitted everything he wrote to her, saying, "Ever since we have been married I have depended on my wife to go over and revise my manuscripts. I have written scarcely anything in twenty-five years she hasn't edited." She never nagged. She knew how far she might go in guiding a genius husband, as he knew how far to go in teasing or taking issue with a genius wife. "Whenever I have failed to follow her advice," he wrote, "I have always come to regret it. She was right, having better taste." He wrote his great works, including his masterpiece *Huckleberry Finn,* after marriage. He boasted that Livy guided him away from becoming a lifelong "lecturing buffoon" to becoming a novelist, writer, philosopher, and historian.

But happy as they were, that first year together turned into a nightmare of illnesses, mishaps, and deaths among those close to

them. Samuel had in the past experienced the tragedy of death
when his adored younger brother Henry, whom he had influenced
to become a riverman, burned to death in a Pennsylvania steam-
boat disaster. Olivia had never experienced the death of anyone
dear to her until that first year of marriage, when her father was
stricken. She, an expectant mother, went with Mark to Elmira to
nurse the sick man. He seemed to revive, but in August, after two
months of exhausting emotional care, Jervis Langdon died. Livy,
careworn and physically spent, returned to Buffalo with Mark,
having invited a young schoolteacher, Emma Nye, to visit them.
Emma sickened almost immediately with typhoid and after a
month died in their bedroom. All of this proved too much for Livy,
and she gave birth prematurely to a frail boy, Langdon. She herself
remained an invalid through the winter that followed. They sold
their holdings in Buffalo and moved into a rented house in Hartford.

By the beginning of the following year the infant son continued
to be sickly and they moved to Nook Farm, a little Hartford community, where Olivia slowly recovered. Here they built a house of
their own, where they remained for the twenty happiest years of
their life together. He struck out on a rigorous lecture tour, but his
peace of mind was troubled at being separated from her. When
away from each other they continued writing letters every day. She
wrote:

> I do hope that this will be the last season that it will be necessry
> for you to lecture; it is not the way for a husband and wife to live
> if they can possibly avoid it. Separation comes soon enough. . . . I
> don't want to be a worrier. I believe there is nothing that sooner
> ruins the happiness of a family than a worrying woman.[3]

And in another letter:

> I can not and I will not think about your being away from me this
> way every year; it is not half living. If in order to sustain our
> present mode of living you are obliged to do so, then we will
> change our mode of living.[4]

He answered, "Lecturing is hateful, but it must come to an end yet,
and then I'll see my darling whom I love, love, love."

Their happiness knew no limits when Olivia gave birth to a daughter, Susy, in March of that year. But three months after the birth of Susy, a severe blow almost felled them. In June, little Langdon, the white-faced baby with a chronic cough, succumbed to diphtheria and died a few days later. Grief-stricken, the parents took the new baby, Susy, and moved to the seashore for the summer. In the years that followed Susy's birth, two more daughters were born to them: Clara two years later, and Jean four years after. The three girls became the joy of their adoring parents. Olivia Clemens was a model mother, giving the children her time, her care, her teaching, her love and tender strictness, while at the same time pouring out her devotion on her husband and his writing. Mark was an ideal father, romping with the children, playing games with them, acting with them, and spoiling them all he could. But he never subordinated his love for Livy to his love for the girls. "It takes a character of vast proportions," wrote Petrarch, "to be equal to a wife and literature both"—to which might be added, "and to three daughters." Mark's character had vast proportions.

The Clemenses had become very wealthy and Mark Twain had become a world-popular and esteemed writer. The family traveled together many times to almost every country in the world, crossing the Atlantic and Pacific numerous times, as invited guests of kings and European rulers. They met and were entertained by every famous author, actor, and political figure in Europe and America. The Prince of Wales (later Edward VII) counted them his friends, as did presidents of the United States—Grant, Garfield, Cleveland, Roosevelt, and their wives. Ministers, priests, and rabbis became their friends and guests. It was indeed the noonday of their success and happiness, and there seemed nothing to challenge their love and devotion to each other. Their friends and acquaintances were so numerous that their daughter Jean, half in pride, half in annoyance, said, "Why, Papa, if this goes on, pretty soon there won't be anybody left for you to meet except God."

Their happiness together seemed unassailable, blessed with financial affluence and a pleasing life-style. Readers throughout the world were demanding more and more from Mark Twain, who was at the height of his creative powers. Their estates were always filled with animals of all sorts and breeds, especially cats. ("I cannot resist a cat," he told them.) Above all, Olivia and Samuel were seldom separated. Mark sang, not just at home, but whenever and wherever the mood came upon him. Once while visiting friends, sitting in the shadowy parlor, moonlight streaming in through the large window, Mark suddenly began to sing, his voice "soft like a faint sound just as if there was a wind in the trees: *Nobody knows the trouble I got, nobody knows but Jesus.*" When he got to the end, to the *Glory,* he stood up and shouted, "Glory, Glory, Hallelujah!"

He was not always singing, to be sure. He was possessed of a violent temper, an urge to swear and curse and rail against the whole "damned human race!" Livy did not hesitate to reprove him for overstepping the bounds of fairness, justice, and taste. Susy, who at the age of thirteen began a biography of her beloved father, tells how the family coped with his bad tempers, his cursing. Livy would give him a treatment they called "Dusting off Papa." The girls would chime in, calling him "the spitting gray kitten ... a kitten with its fur all ruffled." He loved them for the "dusting-off," laughed, begged their forgiveness, promised not to curse and swear again—and went right on swearing. He was strict with the children too, his own version of strictness, more medieval than modern. When he did not approve of one of Clara's suitors, he locked her in a closet "to put sense in her head." Fortunately he left most of the discipline of the children in the hands of Livy, for he realized his shortcomings in certain matters.

In her biography of her father Susy wrote that he did not like to go to church because he couldn't bear to hear anyone talk but himself, that he could listen to himself talk for hours without getting tired. She said her mother would take to her sickbed just so she would not have to listen any more to his cursing about "the damned human race." Susy also noted that "Pa was an awful man before Mama took him in hand and married him." Elsewhere she wrote, "The difference between Mama and Papa is Mama loves religion and Papa loves cats." In describing her father's appearance, she said, "He is an extraordinarily fine looking man." She once asked her mother to see his love letters to her; she refused, saying they were private, but assured Susy they were the most beautiful love letters in the whole world. Susy once asked her, "Mama, if Papa dies will you die too?" and Livy answered, "Unfortunately, no."

Eventually the family lost their fortune because of Mark's bad investments, their lavish spending, his poor business sense, and their inability to refuse great financial aid to struggling musicians, students, and artists. But above all, it was the financial crisis in the country resulting from the panic of 1893 that led Mark Twain to bankruptcy and an indebtedness of over $100,000. Livy would not hear of his taking advantage of the bankruptcy laws, insisting that his creditors be paid 100 cents on the dollar. She would rather be poor, she said, than have his good name as the foremost literary figure in America scandalized and dragged through the courts.

Of course, there was no danger of their being poor; Mark Twain's earning potential never diminished. He undertook lecturing again, and with his continued output of writing and the steady flow of royalties—and with the aid of what remained of Livy's inheritance—within a few years every cent of the debt was paid off. They continued living on the grand scale they were accustomed to. It was something else that felled them. The love which had grown through all those years when "he was fortune's darling and she the little heiress of Elmira" was put to the test of tragic adversity.

In her early twenties Susy showed signs of nervous disorder, and a year or two later she fell gravely ill; high fever, prostration, and a distraught manner forecast the onset of delirium. Her illness was diagnosed as spinal meningitis. She stayed at Quarry Farm, cared for by a doctor, Uncle Charley, and a servant, Katy. Mark, Livy, and Clara were in England when they received news of Susy's illness. Mother and daughter set sail for America; Mark remained in order to find a suitable house for the family, never doubting they would be together again soon. In the Hartford house, Susy grew worse, pacing the floor in a raging fever. The infection crept deeper into her brain and she could no longer see, mistaking Katy for her mother.

But her mother and sister were still in mid-ocean on the evening of August 18 when Susy died. Mark received a cable, but Livy did not learn the sad news until she landed, three days later. Mark, unable to get back in time for the funeral, wrote to Livy: "I know what misery is, at last, my darling. I know what I shall suffer when you die. . . . We have lost her and our life is bitter. We may find her again . . . let us not despair of it . . . but we still have each other, my darling, and this is riches. . . ."[5]

It was he who ordered Susy's gravestone and wrote what is now carved on the granite:

Olivia Susan Clemens
Died August 18, age 24

Warm summer sun shine kindly here;
Warm Southern wind, blow softly here;
Green sod above, lie light, lie light—
Good-night, dear heart, good-night, good-night.[6]

After Susy's death her grieving parents clung to the hope of personal immortality. He cried out to Livy, "Let us believe it, Livy, let us believe it! There is no sense in the universe if death must end all."

During the next eight years Mark and Livy were together almost constantly. He experienced seasons of productivity. "Incessant work," he said, "is my best medicine against the deadness which invaded me when Susy died." They returned to New York in the autumn of 1900. Mark was given a hero's welcome; there was rejoicing that their beloved Mark Twain had come home.

Then a new anxiety assailed the family. Shortly after Susy's death Jean began to show erratic behavior, and, at age sixteen, her condition was diagnosed as epilepsy. A few months later she grew worse. Almost at the same time, Livy became critically ill, her goiter condition and heart disease having adverse effects on each other.

They settled in a house in Riverdale, where Clara (who would soon marry the pianist Ossip Gabrilowitsch) nursed her mother during times of critical illness. On Christmas Eve Jean was down with pneumonia, and then with measles. Livy was put to bed and was told she could have no visitors. Mark, too, was included in this prohibition, but was told he might visit her a few minutes a day, and say good-night to her in the evening. He wrote notes to her and pushed them under the door for the nurse to give to her. In his notebook he wrote, "On our thirty-third wedding anniversary I was allowed to see Livy five minutes this morning in honor of the day." To her he wrote, "I love you darling old-young sweetheart of my youth and my age, and I kiss you good-night."

In October Livy seemed strong enough for the family to sail for Florence, Italy. They rented a villa, hoping that the sun of Italy would help her recover, but there was no sun and Livy grew weaker. Again Mark was permitted only a few minutes a day with her, as had been the rule in Riverdale. Unable to bear being separated from her, he broke the rule often, slipping into the room during the day just for a glimpse of her. "She'd put her arms around his neck," Katy told Mark's biographer, "the first thing, and he'd hold her soft, and give her one of them tender kisses. . . . It was a great love, I tell you."

Livy wanted a home of her own and they kept up the pretense of searching for a villa or a house that would be suitable. She seemed to be recovering, took an excited interest in their househunting, in Clara's successful singing concert, in family news, in everything. Mark went out at night pinning notes on trees, telling the birds not to sing so loudly because Livy was ill. She looked so young, so bright, so pretty to him that he wrote a note about her seeming recovery, but immediately added in a superstitious fear that he was inviting evil: "It won't last and I shall go back to my prayers again." She was feeling better, though, and she invited him to sit by her, talk to her, tell her about everything. He stayed too long and the nurse insisted he leave. "You'll come back?" she asked. He said, "Yes, to say good-night." He went upstairs, sat down at the piano and sang an old Jubilee song—one that Susy liked to hear him sing: *Swing Low, Sweet Chariot.* Jean came into the room to listen, and he sang again, *My Lord He Calls Me.* Livy heard him singing and said to the nurse, "He is singing a good-night carol to me."

At 9:30 he came in to say good-night. A little group was gathered around the bed. Clara and Jean were standing there, half-dazed. Mark approached the bed, bent over and looked at Livy, surprised that she did not greet him. Clara and Jean cried, "Oh, Katy, is it true? Is it true?" Only then did Mark Twain know that his wife was dead.

They took her body back to America on the *Prince Oscar.* Aboard the ship he wrote in his notebook: "In thirty-four years we have made many voyages together, Livy dear, and now we are making our last; you down below and lonely. I above with the crowd and lonely." She was buried in Elmira, and once again he wrote an epitaph for a loved one: her name, date of birth, date of death, followed by a German line, *"Gott sei dir gnädig, O meine Wonne!"* (God be gracious to you, O my rapture!).

For five years after Olivia's death Mark Twain and his daughter Jean were alone. Clara, now married, was living in Europe with her husband. Father and daughter moved to a beautiful house, *Stormfield,* at Redding, Connecticut. In those five years Mark had grown closer to this daughter than he had ever been before. They took trips together, and the one they took to Bermuda was wonderfully refreshing for both. They returned around Christmas time, both "flushed with splendid health." They ate dinner and afterwards strolled hand in hand to the library, where they sat and chatted and planned the future until nine o'clock—which was late for them. From her youth Jean had been the only daughter Mark felt needed to be given religious faith, to be convinced that a strong faith is the only antidote against despair. Mark had written to Olivia (when Jean was still a young girl):

> I am very glad Jean is in a Catholic convent. . . . And away deep down in my heart I feel that if they make a good strong unshakable Catholic of her I shan't be the least bit sorry. It is doubtless the most peace giving and restful of all the religions. If I had it I would not trade it for anything on earth.[7]

Now, as they were parting for the night, he felt that Jean was giving him the antidote against his despair. At his door Jean said, "I can't kiss you, Father; I have a cold and you could catch it." He bent and kissed her hand, and she impulsively kissed his hand in return.

At half-past seven in the morning he awoke and heard voices outside his door. Katy entered. She was quaking, her voice gasping, "Miss Jean is dead!" He went immediately to Jean's room. She lay on the floor in the bathroom covered by a sheet. She had had an epileptic seizure with a convulsion and heart attack, and had died in her bath.

For the third time he wrote an epitaph for one of his loved ones, giving her name, the date of her birth, the date of her death, her age, twenty-nine. Underneath was carved, "After life's fitful fever she sleeps well." It was the last epitaph he would have to write—

Clara would be the only one to survive him. Letters about Jean's death, written for Clara, were the last great things he wrote. The last book he read, day after day until he finished it, was Thomas Hardy's *Jude the Obscure,* a novel that is the story of love and marriage, a story of belief and unbelief, of the fleeting nature of dreams and ambitions, and, above all, the story of the death of children.

Mark Twain was born in 1835 as Halley's comet streaked across the sky. He had predicted he would die when the comet returned—and he did. Mark Twain died in 1910, as Halley's comet reappeared in its predicted orbit. A nation and the world mourned him as he was buried next to his wife in the Elmira cemetery. In death, as in life, Samuel and Olivia Clemens were together.

5

Nora and James Joyce

Biographies of James Joyce invariably reveal Nora, his wife, as an unappreciative mate, not an inspiration. Certain it is that she never responded kindly to Joyce's writing. She was hostile to his strange style, as was the general, nonelite reading public.

Joyce longed for her encouragement in his work, but he would not change. He was inwardly compelled to report his experience of life, and his experience reflected a world, a society, the whole of Western culture, disintegrating. To express this disintegration he struck at the root—language. Yet, paradoxically enough, he did not tackle the basic institution, monogamy. On the contrary, he idealized the monogamous union of a man and a woman, provided it was rooted and grounded in love—romantic love. His famous novel *Ulysses,* a classic of modern literature, is a story of monogamous marriage, a sacramental union of a man and a woman who clung to the ideal of an eternal vow.

The Belgian Nobel laureate scientist Ilya Prigogine says that disequilibrium is more natural and affirmative than equilibrium. Equilibrium, so comforting to humans, is really stagnation. Disequilibrium is the catalyst for new life. Nora brought to her union

64

with James Joyce the disequilibrium out of which was born a new life, indeed, a new creative mode of expression that affected not only literature, but all the arts, including music and painting.

Their meeting was romantic—a June evening in Dublin. The young Irishman caught up with the redhaired girl he was following, and tipped his cap—a yachting cap. Nora joked that she took him for a Swedish sailor because of his pale blue eyes. He walked with her to her place of employment, Finn's Hotel, and asked to see her again. She agreed, but when he arrived at the appointed place, she was not there. He never forgot the date—June 14. He thought that she had heard of his bad reputation as "a lewd-spoken youth" and a "familiar of night town." Also, he was already known as a drinking man, though so young. He went home and wrote to her. "I may be blind. I looked for a long time at a head of reddish brown hair and decided it was not yours. I went home quite dejected. I would like to make an appointment, but it might not suit you. I hope you will be kind enough to make one with me—if you have not forgotten me! James A. Joyce, 15 June 1904."[1]

The next day, June 16, she met him and they went for a walk. It was the beginning of their long walk through life together. When Joyce wrote *Ulysses* he opened it on the fateful day that changed his life and hers—June 16—because, said he, "it was a sacred day."

Nora always said that she came from ordinary people (unlike Jim, whose family was extraordinary). Her father, a baker, was also a drinking man, who kept the family poor. When Nora's mother, already with a large brood, was once again pregnant, she sent five-year-old Nora to her grandmother. The child was sent to a convent school, where she received an orphan's education. "Nora, handsome, jaunty, daring and untutored, was destined to join her life with one of the rarefied minds of the century,"[2] wrote a biographer.

Nora affected Jim profoundly from the first instant, as his letters to her reveal. Although his signature was formal (either "Mr. Joyce" or "J.A.J."), the contents were not: "I came in at half past eleven. Since then I have been sitting in an easy chair like a fool. I could do nothing. I hear nothing but your voice. I am like a fool hearing you call me 'Dear.' "

In another letter Jim wrote, "When I am with you I leave aside my contemptuous suspicious nature. . . . Will you write something to me? I hope you will. How am I to sign myself? I won't sign anything at all, because I don't know what to sign myself. 15 August 1904."[3]

Jim had never been in love, and his feelings for Nora were so different from his other experiences of crude sexuality that he amazed his bohemian friends. They were disgusted and shocked that Joyce, formerly a rebel against all traditions, had fallen in love like this, wanting to bind this girl to himself forever. As for Jim, he was sure Nora was meant to be his, for better and for worse. But he felt he had to test her, to make sure she loved him enough to take him with all his vices and faults. One night he confessed to her what his sexual life had been before he met her. Though Nora was described as a flirtatious girl, everyone who knew her was impressed by a certain basic simplicity. "Nora was both flirtatious and innocent," her friends said.

She was shocked by Jim's confession, and thought he surely must not respect her to tell her these things about himself. A biographer of Chesterton described him "as a schoolboy with his brooding on doubts and dirt and daydreams, of crude conscientiousness so inconsistent as to be near hypocrisy." The same could be said of James Joyce. They were young men of their era, an era in which puritanism and a shallow idea of respectability ("What will people think?") distorted nature and instinct. Religion suffered under the narrowness of society's attitudes, and its stress was not on compassion, but on hellfire and damnation.

Joyce told his friend Padraic Colum that as a lad he had envisioned entering the Jesuit order, where he had been educated. Then in adolescence he went through a violent religious crisis: "Mind you, it was not a question of belief. It was a question of celibacy. I knew I could not live as a celibate."[4]

Jim wrote Nora a letter explaining himself further: "I may have pained you tonight by what I said. . . . My mother was slowly killed, I think, by my father's ill-treatment, by years of trouble, and by my cynical frankness of conduct." He begged her not to be shy of him because he had confessed his sins, but to absolve him out of love. "I saw in you an extraordinary melancholy tenderness. . . . I understood that in your eyes I was inferior to a convention of our present society." But he asked that she look beneath all his masks and see his real simplicity and basic innocence. "No human being has ever stood so close to my soul as you stand. . . . I want more than your caresses."[5]

His intent was never to be separated from her, yet he dared not tell his father. His father would look down on "a Galway girl of no family." There was nothing to do but elope and leave Ireland. Penniless, Jim petitioned his good friend J. F. Byrne for a loan. When Byrne asked Jim if he was really sincere, he replied, "She's the only girl I will ever love." At that, Byrne declared, "Then ask Nora and if she agrees, go away immediately." And he gave him the loan.

Jim went directly to Nora, who said yes. Then he went home and put the proposal to her in writing, so she would have a very real token of his seriousness. "It seemed to me that I was fighting a battle with every religious and social force in Ireland for you . . . that you can choose to stand beside me in this way in my hazardous life fills me with great pride and joy . . . ."[6]

Jim had already written to the Berlitz School in London, asking for a teaching job in Europe, so he and Nora went off to London. There he took her to a park and asked her to wait. He had run out of money and had to go to friends for another loan. Nora waited— for two hours. At last he returned with more funds.

Mary Colum wrote that Jim was very middle-class about love and marriage:

> Joyce had not any of what are called Bohemian qualities. . . .
> He was scrupulously moral and ethically above reproach. In spite of his visits to Nighttown in his student and post student days in Dublin, he had fixed ideas of faithfulness in marriage, and nothing shocked him more than to hear that somebody he knew was committing adultery. . . . He had strong convictions about matrimony . . . .[7]

They went from London directly to Paris, where Jim once more had to leave Nora in a park waiting while he went in search of friends from whom to borrow more money. He had been told a post was open at the Berlitz school in Zurich. Finally they made it to Zurich and were directed to Gasthaus Hoffnung. "Here for the first time since their elopement they were by themselves, and Joyce retained a special feeling for the dingy hotel where he and Nora first consummated their love."

Unfortunately, it turned out that there was no Zurich job. They were told to try Trieste. There Joyce at last found work as a teacher at the Berlitz school, and they had enough money to rent a miserable furnished room with kitchen on the third floor of a house near the school. But they were left impoverished after paying the rent and had to borrow paraffin for their lamp; the room had no stove.

While Jim went out to teach, Nora sat in the dingy room waiting for him to return, lonely and bewildered. The language was strange, and even when Jim came home, he seemed strange. He went immediately to the table to write. Then he would read the chapters he had written aloud to her. She couldn't make them out at all, and asked him with her characteristic candor why he was wasting all that paper.

Jim began his long complaint to his friends, one continuing over all the years of their marriage, that Nora cared nothing for his art, did not understand that he was not an ordinary person. He decided that he had to try to educate her, and read her modern stories by other experimental writers. When he finished one of the stories, she shook her head: "That man doesn't know how to end a story."

But Nora wished Jim had not gone into writing. He had a beautiful tenor voice. "Jim should have stuck to music instead of bothering with writing," she often said. Padraic Colum—the Colums were their closest friends—also spoke of Jim's voice as extraordinary: "Joyce's voice was unlike any other singer's—humorous, sorrowful, it was unforgettable."[8] But he did not agree with Nora that Jim should throw away the pen and go into singing. As for their other artist and writer friends, they were exasperated with Nora, and felt that Jim had made a bad mistake. "It won't last," they predicted.

Joyce told them all that he was like Blake and would remold Nora's soul until it was a "creation of his own"—but at the same time he did not want Nora to change. He loved her precisely because she was so different from him. When he got too serious about remolding her soul, she would joke with him and suggest he was trying too hard, because "he had a beautiful character and a saint's face." This would take him down, and he would immediately deny both accusations, saying that he had a poor character and "the face of a great sinner."

Trieste summers are hot, and the Joyces' miserable room became intolerable. Nora, who was pregnant, was constantly in tears. "I do not know what strange morose creature she will bring forth after all her tears," he told his friends who took him out to drink and forget his troubles. He wrote his brother Stanislaus, asking him to find them a small cottage in the Dublin suburbs so that Nora would be happier. But suddenly, before a cottage could be found, the child, a son was born. When the baby boy was put in his arms, Jim forgot all his troubles and began to sing; then he hurried out to send a cable to Stanislaus: "Son born Jim." They named the baby Giorgio, and Joyce wrote to his sister Eva, "The most important thing that can happen to a man is the birth of a child . . . being a father brings hope and love in the world."[9]

The hero of Joyce's novel *Ulysses*, Leopold Bloom, is supposed to be the ideal husband and father. He is a Jew "baptized into both the Protestant and Catholic Church." Ellmann, in his biography of James Joyce, declares that "Bloom unites in himself the Greek-Jewish-Irishman . . . the cultures seem to unite against horsepower and brutality in favor of brainpower and decency . . . the eternal affirmation of the spirit of man. . . . In making his hero Leopold Bloom, Joyce recognized implicitly what he often spoke of directly, his affinity for Jews as a wandering, persecuted people. 'I sometimes think,' he said . . . 'that it was a heroic sacrifice on their part when they refused to accept the Christian revelation. Look at them. They are better husbands than we are, better fathers and better sons. . . .'"[10]

Jim idealized both marriage and Nora, sometimes comparing her to Mary, for whom he had never lost his devotion, even when he abandoned the Catholic Church. Reading Dante, he found another genius whose wife had been unsympathetic to his writings; yet that marriage, too, was ideal as far as Joyce was concerned. "I love Dante almost as much as the Bible," he said. The more he thought about Dante, the closer he felt to him in all ways, for he, too, was an exile. But Joyce realized that Dante had had to go into exile without his wife and children and that he was fortunate to have Nora and Giorgio. This insight made him decide to abandon his habit of leaving her alone in the evenings while he went to the cafe to drink with his friends. He began inviting them home, and Nora happily entertained them with humorous remarks. They would play with Giorgio and sing all night. Brother Stanislaus came to Trieste to live with them and teach at the Berlitz school also. He saw that despite all their quarrels, Jim and Nora were ideally suited to each other, throve on their hectic family life. Crying babies, diapers hanging on strings in the kitchen, piles of manuscript on rickety tables, made no difference. Joyce himself wrote a story depicting their home:

> A drafty little stone-flagged room, chest of drawers to left . . . in the centre, a small table on which are writing materials . . . in the background, small-sized bed. A young man with snivelling nose sits at the table; on the bed sit a madonna and a plaintive infant. . . . Title of above: The Anarchist."[11]

Meanwhile Nora was pregnant again and insisted they had to find better living quarters. This problem drove Joyce to drink more heavily. One night he was followed home from the cafe, knocked down, and robbed of a month's paycheck. It was the last straw for Nora. She said she was going home to Dublin. Jim didn't think poverty could be the reason. He suspected that she wanted to go back to Dublin to visit the grave of one of her old suitors. In anguish Jim wrote her a note: "Why is it that words seem to me so dull and cold? Is it because there is no word tender enough to be your name?"

Nora was reconciled, and they both agreed that the best thing to do was to get away from bad company, to leave Trieste. They went to Rome, where Jim got a job as bank clerk, which he detested. They returned to Trieste and immediately he fell in with his old companions, going once more to the cafe every night and getting drunk. One night he fell into the gutter and became very ill. Taken to the hospital with rheumatic fever, he was not home when Nora went into labor. "The baby was almost born on the street . . . a daughter born July 26 in the pauper ward."[12] They named her Lucia Anne, and once again Jim was ecstatic over the birth of a child. He hoped for a large family. But Nora, soon pregnant again, had a miscarriage and would not be able to bear more children.

Jim grieved, and in *Ulysses* he wrote about the sorrow of a father over an unborn child.

Determined to demonstrate his devotion to his family more dramatically, Jim decided to broach a reconciliation with his father. He took Giorgio to Dublin and brought grandfather and grandson together. His father was delighted and forgave Jim and Nora. But while in Dublin, Joyce ran into a companion of his youth named Cosgrove, who had once been in love with Nora. Cosgrove told Joyce he had been more than friendly with Nora, and Joyce went into a passion of jealousy. He went home and wrote to his wife: "I can see nothing but your face as it was then raised to meet another's. O, Nora pity me for what I suffer now. . . . My faith in that face I loved is broken. O, Nora, Nora have pity for my poor wretched love. . . . I loved you only and you have broken my faith in you."[13] He could not sleep. He paced the streets of Dublin. At last he went to see his old friend Byrne and poured out Cosgrove's story.

"I have never seen a human being more shattered," wrote Byrne later. But Byrne knew that Cosgrove had been waiting his chance to wreck Jim and Nora for years and said his "brag was a blasted lie." Then Joyce came to his senses, recalling that Cosgrove had always been bitterly jealous of him, and in the days of their youth had been prone to play harmful tricks on him.

Meanwhile, however, Jim's letters reached Nora. Stunned and bewildered, she brooded silently for days, not writing, not speaking. Then at last she wrote him a brief note, exposing her own vulnerability, saying that he had already "been too kind to the ignorant girl he had taken up with and ought to separate himself from her."

After Nora had mailed the letter, Stanislaus demanded to know what was wrong. She showed him Jim's letters. Furious, he wrote immediately to his brother. He told Jim that he remembered how Cosgrove had met him one night, years ago, in Dublin, very depressed. Stanislaus had asked him what was wrong, and Cosgrove (swearing Stanislaus to secrecy) said that he had just been rebuffed and sent packing by Nora Barnacle. So, contrary to the man's brag, he had actually suffered a humiliating defeat at Nora's hands, and now was getting revenge.

"My darling, what a worthless fellow I am, but after this I will be worthy of you, dearest. . . . My sweet noble Nora . . . forgive me for my contemptible conduct . . . ,"[14] Jim wrote at once. To his astonishment, she answered immediately, not just forgiving him, but telling him what was sweetest balm to his own wounded heart—that she was reading his poems! So great good had come out of this suffering, Jim declared.

He felt closer to Blake than ever, saying that both of them were geniuses who had married uneducated women out of pure love and found a deeper compatibility. He decided that Blake must have been an Irishman—they were so alike, they had the same spirituality, the same socialism based on the Beatitudes, the same love of children. He believed that he was a mystic like Blake, whom he referred to as "the celestial man." Blake's marriage was an ideal Joyce himself wished to emulate. He told his bohemian friends that *their* love lives were spurious; his was true reality. "I am more virtuous than the lot—I, who am a real monogamist and have never loved but once in my life."[15]

Yet Nora and Jim would never be serene and peaceful lovers. He kept on drinking, and in his book *Ulysses,* he decided to portray Molly, Bloom's wife, as having many lovers. But at the same time, Joyce implied that it was all in Bloom's imagination. "If Molly were really promiscuous in her conduct, Joyce would not have used her for his heroine," says Ellmann. Joyce was writing about his own inner conflicts, the agonies of jealousy he seemed to indulge. Joyce believed that the artist and his life are not distinct, the artist is his work, and his life is his fiction.

World War I uprooted the family from Zurich. Friends worried about them, especially since Jim was having severe eye trouble requiring surgery. When they wrote asking how he was, Nora, who hated to write letters, didn't answer. Even when Jim begged her to write a word of thanks to friends who sent loans, she would not. Nora's attitude seemed to result, in part, from an incident early in their romance. Jim had begged her to write to him; she did. Later she learned he had read her letter to friends who criticized it as stilted and "ordinary." She never wrote letters again, except in great emergencies. Sometimes Joyce bragged about his knowledge of feminine psychology. Nora would quietly mutter, "He knows nothing at all about women."

Jim's fame was increasing, and patrons of the arts made grants of money available to the Joyces. Ezra Pound, who was instrumental in helping them in this way, insisted they come to live in Paris, where friends could keep an eye on them. On July 8, 1920, the Joyces arrived for a week's stay and remained for twenty years.

There at last the great book James Joyce had been working on was published. On February 2, 1922, his fortieth birthday, they celebrated with friends. Jim opened the package of books, took out the first copy, inscribed it and handed it to Nora. Arthur Power, a friend, sitting next to her, cried out, "Now Nora's copy is worth a fortune!" Humorously, Nora offered to sell it to him. Jim didn't think she was funny. "Open the book and read it! Look at the date on which the story opens!"[16] She did, but drew a blank. He had to explain that June 16, 1904, the beginning of the story of *Ulysses*, commemorated his first walk with Nora Barnacle.

Friends assured him that Nora might not appreciate his book, but the notables of the world did. T. S. Eliot wrote, "With *Ulysses* Joyce killed the nineteenth century." Alas, Nora liked the nineteenth century, both its stories and its songs. Others felt as she did. Even the supposedly revolutionary George Bernard Shaw wrote, "I could not write the words Mr. Joyce uses: my prudish hand would refuse to form the letters; and I find no interest in his infantile clinical incontinences, or in the flatulences which he thinks worth mentioning. . . . Joyce is driven by his documentary demon to place on record the working of a young man's imagination for a single day in the environment of Dublin . . . the Dublin Jackeens of my day, the medical students, the young bloods about town, were very like that. Their conversation was dirty. . . . I should like to organize the young men of Dublin into clubs for the purpose of reading *Ulysses;* so that they could debate the question: 'Are we like that?' "[17]

H. G. Wells wrote to him: "I've enormous respect for your genius. . . ." Indeed, the publication of *Ulysses* created a Joyce cult. In Paris he was treated as a shrine. "Pilgrims came to the new shrine." All except Nora. Everybody who was anybody, who belonged to the elite, was reading *Ulysses*—except his wife. Yet this great modern classic about marriage had been brought forth because of her.

In *Ulysses*, a marriage is purged of evil through love. Ellmann says *Ulysses* is an "epithalamium. . . . The spirit is liberated from its bonds through a eucharistic occasion, an occasion characterized by the joy that, even as a young man, Joyce had praised as the emotion in comedy which makes it a higher form than tragedy. . . . The theme of *Ulysses* is simple . . . it is love."[18]

The monumental work born of Jim and Nora's marriage was intended to extol monogamy. Ironically, however, they did not live in peace. They quarreled bitterly over his drinking and his writing. He was bitter because she would not read *Ulysses;* she was bitter because he would not stop drinking. One time she even took the children and left for Ireland. Jim fired off telegrams to her: "My darling, my love, my queen . . . it is impossible to describe to you the despair I have been in since you left." At the news that the doctors were going to operate again on his eyes, Nora brought the children home immediately. "They flew into each other's arms like bride and bridegroom," wrote brother Stanislaus disgustedly.

But Nora hadn't changed. She told her sister exasperatedly, "He's on another book again"—as if it were a vice. And she went on making remarks to their friends: "I've always told Jim he should give up writing and take up singing. To think he was once on the same platform with James McCormack."[19]

The book Joyce was writing was *Finnegans Wake.* Parts of it appeared in avant-garde periodicals, and even his literary benefactors, like Ezra Pound, were confused. "I am worried about its incomprehensibility," he said. When Jim heard this, he fell ill and had to go to bed. There he lay, with no appetite for food, just looking forlornly at Nora. "Why don't you write sensible books that people can understand?" she scolded, but went out to find his trustworthy friends. They came to visit the invalid and assured him that "he was not mad, just touched enough for genius in the James Jesus Joyce manner."

Nora and Jim were middle-aged now, but still romantics. Nora, in her mid-forties, had to go into the hospital for exploratory surgery, so Jim went in with her and ordered a bed next to hers. The surgery, followed by radium treatments, didn't help. In February 1929, Nora had a hysterectomy, and again, Jim had a bed placed right next to hers. Both remained in the hospital for a couple of months, and subsequently, Jim had to have more eye surgery. Concerned friends told him, "Nora and the children are unprotected—it would be prudent to be legally married." Jim retorted that they were already married. At last they persuaded him, and the whole family went to London to see Nora and Jim legally wed. But at once Joyce started an argument by telling the clerk he and his wife were already married. Then, said the clerk, they must get divorced before he would marry them a second time. Finally the clerk agreed to make an exception for James and Nora Joyce, and performed the legal ritual.

For some time Lucia had been acting strangely, and upon Jim and Nora's return home she broke down and had to be taken to a sanitarium. The only bright moment in the distraught parents' life was the birth of a grandson. George (Giorgio) and his wife, Helen, named the child Stephen James Joyce. He was baptized secretly— with the connivance of Padraic and Mary Colum—for no one wished to upset Jim, who loved the sacraments but hated the institutional church.

Jim and Nora could not bear to have Lucia in a sanitarium, yet they could not care for her at home. The Swiss psychiatrist Carl Jung, fascinated by Joyce's book, had written to him wanting to analyze him. Never, declared the writer. But at last Jim and Nora were persuaded to send Lucia to Jung in Zurich. From the Institute there she wrote to her parents: "Father dear, I have had too nice a life. I am spoiled. You must both forgive me. So many people were envious of me and Mama, because you are too good."[20]

Lucia seemed to be doing well, but the recovery did not last. Once more they had to place her in a sanitarium. By the nineteen-thirties, their financial difficulties were great, although good royalties were coming in from the American edition of *Ulysses*. This time it was not Nora and Jim's wild extravagance, but simply the fact that three-quarters of their income went to care for Lucia.

The Monster, as Joyce now called *Finnegans Wake*, was finally finished, and arrived on January 30 in time for his February 2 birthday. He gave Nora a ring set with an aquamarine to symbolize "the Liffey," which was the river of memory in the book.

Just as the book came out, the war exploded over Europe. Jim and Nora would have to be wanderers and exiles once more. Their worry was for Lucia: "She must not be left alone in terror, believing she is abandoned by everybody in case of a bombardment in Paris," Joyce wrote importunately to the doctors, seeking to get her settled in a safe place. They realized that Zurich was the only place for all of them. Thanks to the help of influential friends, they were able, after many complications, to obtain visas.

On December 17, 1940 the family left for Zurich, the city where he and Nora had come thirty-six years earlier, full of hope. Now their worn faces were marked by troubles and sorrows. In 1904 he and Nora had been nobodies; now the hotel where they had consummated their sacrament of love had been renamed—from Gasthaus Hoffnung to Gasthause Doeblin.

A week after Christmas Jim became very ill; he recovered but two weeks later he was taken to the hospital in an ambulance, to be operated on for a perforated duodenal ulcer. Nora moved into the room with him, just as he had done with her.

After surgery on a Friday, he seemed to be recovering well, but on Sunday morning he sank into a coma. A few moments later he came out of the coma to ask for Nora and told her to move her bed closer to his. Then he sank into the coma again. She moved her bed right next to his, but the doctors told her he would be in a coma for days, that her presence was a hindrance to them, and that she herself was exhausted. Promising to telephone her if there was any change, the nurses persuaded George to take her home.

At one in the morning Joyce awoke. He told the nurse to call Nora, but she did not get around to it until two. When Nora and George arrived, Jim was dead.

Years earlier, a French photographer had made an appointment to take pictures of James Joyce. When she arrived, after having taken many pictures of Joyce, she asked Nora to pose with him. Nora would not do it. Jim asked her at least to pose with him for family pictures. The woman begged, but Nora was adamant. "I'm nobody," she said.

There are many pictures of James Joyce and very few of Nora. But her looks, her quality, are captured in the words written by friends. "Nora Joyce wore a scarlet shawl that set off her abundant graying hair, fine eyes, and good features . . . she was not only beautiful but vivacious and humorous . . . ," wrote the Colums. "James Joyce was markedly devoted to Nora; her personality was full of interest to him, and he delighted in her sayings. . . . Once, when I called to see Nora, I found him crumpled up in delight at something she was saying, speaking of a slummy apartment a writer friend used, she said: 'That place is not fit to wash a rat in. . . .' "[21]

"She never read his books and with a total disregard for posterity, she tore up many of his letters to her," wrote another friend of the Joyces, who went on to say that Nora defended her actions, declaring, "They were just for me."

6

Paula and Martin Buber

The twentieth century brought with it many of the political upheavals, wars, and threats of war that the nineteenth century had been unable, even unwilling, to settle. Two World Wars, religious hatred, and holocaust dominated the epoch. It hardly seemed a period in which the Judaeo-Christian ideal of marriage could reach an apogee. But two marriages in particular exemplify the phenomenon of enduring mystical, romantic relationship: the marriage of Martin Buber to Paula Winkler (he a Jew, she a Christian) and that of Jacques Maritain to Raissa Oumansoff (he a Christian, she a Jew).

During his sixty years of marriage to Paula, Martin Buber became one of the most influential philosophers of the twentieth century. In 1965, aged eighty-seven, he died in Jerusalem in their house on Lovers of Zion Street. Seven years earlier in 1958, eighty-one-year-old Paula Buber, had been stricken with pneumonia aboard a boat on its way to Israel, had died at Lido, Venice. Their marriage, it has been written, is a love story in which the "lovers are present for all time unto death and after."

At his eighty-fifth birthday party, Martin Buber visited with a few friends in his warm, book-filled study. A grandchild brought

78

tea and cakes for the guests. Martin was old and bent; nevertheless his voice was clear and strong, and his "conversation was alive with wisdom"—so the guests later recalled the birthday visit. All day long, from all over the world, tributes had been arriving: telegrams, gifts, baskets of fruit, flowers, and expressions of love personally delivered. Martin, a small, delicate man with clear blue eyes and patriarchal white beard, accepted the honors paid him without false humility, but with the kindly humor his students were familiar with.

When the guests left, members of Martin's family—his son, daughter, grandchildren—came home from a luncheon given by the students from the Hebrew University in honor of Professor Buber's birthday. His son told him that the students were planning to serenade him, at midnight; it was a European custom that Martin was well familiar with. Both his son and daughter wondered whether it would be too much for their father, considering the cold temperature and the late hour. But he shook his head: "No, no, let the students come. Paula and I used to join such serenades in Leipsig—except," he laughed, "we did not join many since there were few, very few professors we liked. No, no, let them come."

At midnight some five hundred students, professors, and neighbors carrying burning torches, trumpets blaring, approached the house on Lovers of Zion Street. Many of them crowded into the small garden, where a cypress and palm tree rustled their foliage and fronds in the chilly wind. Martin, wearing a heavy coat against the night air, came out on the porch, followed by the members of his family. The serenaders caught sight of him and a shout went up, followed by the singing of, "Happy birthday, dear Martin!" A young woman came up to him, kissed him on each cheek and placed a garland of flowers around his neck. His eyes wrinkled in a kind of wink: "Is there only one woman student? There should be more, there should be more." The girls and women in the crowd applauded, and another great shout went up from the serenaders. It was over, and when they seemed reluctant to leave, Martin's granddaughter led him back into the warm house.

It was not until after his marriage to Paula that Martin Buber's name and writings became known other than by a very narrow segment of people in Vienna—a fact he was well aware of. He reiterated throughout his life that his meeting with Paula was the great event of his life, that his marriage to her was the "touch-stone" of all he wrote. He intimated that his "forever-marriage" to Paula should be commemorated, not his birthdays.

Martin was born in Vienna on February 8, 1878. His parents were middle-class Jews, and his father was neither religious nor particularly intellectual. He knew very little about his mother, for when he was three years old his mother and father separated. It was a shattering upheaval in the child's life. He was later to tell Paula that the separation of his parents was the first intimation he had that "life was not always idyllic; that life was sometimes tragic." He went to live with his grandparents who, even though they were good to him, refused (because the father commanded it) to talk or answer questions about his mother. Whenever he asked about her, he was told, without explanation, that she was not coming back anymore. A feeling of deprivation, of loss, saddened his childhood, and when he was thirteen he coined a word for his feeling: "a-meeting-that-had-gone-wrong."

In his old age he told an interviewer, "When I was thirty-three I saw my mother again, for the first time in thirty years. The coined word flashed through my mind; this was a meeting that had gone wrong. Whatever I have learned in the course of my life about the meaning of meeting and dialogue between persons springs from that moment when I was three."[1]

At age seventeen he enrolled at the University of Vienna. He was uncertain what he wanted to study or what he wanted to make of his life. He felt alone, but refused to indulge in self-pity. He was a slight youth, below the average height, peaceful by nature, and, being a Jew, he was not befriended by most of the other students. He understood their "otherness" and would have loved to engage them in a dialogue about the beauty and profundity of "differences," but they did not seem interested in his "otherness."

Alone, he would walk the streets of Vienna; then, one day, as he was walking home from the university, he witnessed something that caused him to think twice about remaining in Vienna: A group of Polish students were beating up two defenseless, smaller, Jewish students. Martin felt helpless to intervene. He wanted to talk to someone about anti-Semitism, about the impossibility of believing in a vengeful God, which his grandfather's teachings about Judaism suggested, but there was no one to whom he might talk. Christianity with violent Christians was false; Judaism with a God of vengeance was false; Vienna was false.

Martin was to enroll in other universities during his student and teaching years—Berlin, Zurich, Frankfurt—but when he left Vienna for Leipzig it was at the large university there that an important change in his life took place. The intellectual and cultural atmosphere was not confined to the university itself; Martin experienced it throughout Leipzig. He wandered the narrow streets of the old town, contemplating the sixteenth-century houses with their high-pitched roofs. He visited Auerbach's *Hof,* which he knew from having read and studied Goethe's *Faust.* He visited the thirteenth-century citadel where Martin Luther in 1519 had held his historic "disputation." In the inner town, he liked best to visit the large Church of St. Thomas (Thomaskirche) because Johann Sebastian Bach had once been organist there, and his music was still played there almost daily on the great organ. But Leipzig was destined to have more than aesthetic significance for Martin; it was the place where his meeting with Paula Winkler took place.

Paula was born in Munich and grew up in a devout Catholic family. When barely out of her teens, she left home, not only to attend university, but to live in an artists' colony among writers and artists. While at the university she made a brilliant record in the humanities, read and studied the German mystics, and involved herself wholly in the movements for justice, freedom, compassion, and brotherhood which sprang up among the university students in opposition to the rising waves of anti-Semitism that were threatening to inundate the world. At the time she met Martin she was a small, fair-skinned, slender girl, barely twenty-one, highly intelligent. Martin, who himself had just turned twenty-one, described her as being like an elfin spirit. Both were students at the university, two individuals of different backgrounds, a Jew and a Catholic, involving themselves in the same humane causes.

The year was 1899, and the times had turned ugly, politically and morally. Religious bigotry seemed to have hardened the hearts of humanity. In Martin Buber's words, an "eclipse of God" was taking place. Jews, in particular, were being expelled from Russia, Austria, France, and Germany. No country would accept the thousands of refugees driven from their homelands. However, by 1896 a movement had already been started to establish in Palestine a legally assured home. The movement was initiated by Theodor Herzl, who also founded a newspaper, *Die Welt,* dedicated to the need for a Jewish homeland. In 1899 Martin Buber was appointed editor of *Die Welt.* One of his writers on the paper was the Catholic Paula Winkler.

They were drawn to each other, physically and intellectually, and married soon after they met. She continued to work with him on *Die Welt* with complete dedication to what was now being termed "the Jewish cause." As with everything she and Martin encountered in life, they were giving themselves fully to the struggle for a homeland in Palestine, to the hope for peace with justice for Jew and Arab in "Zion." For Paula, giving of herself wholly to the persecuted Jews was not merely a matter of dialogue, nor a simple matter of lending her support; she had to "become the dialogue herself," she had to become one with the encountered, one with Martin too. She converted to Judaism, an act for which her family cut her off completely; Martin's people became her people, his God her God. Like Ruth in the Bible, Paula for the rest of her life was "an alien in their midst."

Martin and Paula knew the risks involved in a mixed marriage but faced them with responsibility. One of the tenets of Martin Buber's philosophy was the need for understanding the otherness of persons encountered. "Experiencing the *other* is the essence of love," he wrote. "The turning of the lover to the beloved in his otherness, means seeing the other as present for all time." Marriage for him and for Paula had nothing to do with "a meaningful relationship"; marriage, as the exemplary bond, was a decisive union, a risk taken responsibly. It was a risk not merely because she was a Christian and he a Jew, but because she had a different way of thinking, "a different perception of the world, a different faith, coming from a different soil."

With complete openness they affirmed the differences. Paradoxically, their otherness led them to sameness. Their differences opened to them vistas of life neither had encountered before. Their interest in the Palestinian homeland never weakened, but they were just as passionately open to every new meeting. They worked together, studied together, traveled together, tested their ideas on each other. All through their marriage Martin depended on Paula. She accompanied him everywhere, on his lecture tours, whenever he traveled to receive various honors, up to the day of her death. When she was stricken she was returning with him from a lecture tour in the United States. She introduced him to the German mystics, and to Jesus. He became fired, through her, by Christian mysticism. He introduced her to Hasidism—to those joyful Jewish mystics who spoke directly to God as a person in an I-Thou relationship, whose prayer-life included a believing humanism. "Their belief and way of life," she said, "is like the belief and way of life of the early Christians." She, with Martin, delved deeply into the legends about the Baal-shem, the joyful, mystical founder of Hasidism.

Martin and Paula were twenty-six when they decided to go into isolation together to write a book on Hasidism. The book, *The Tales of the Hasidim,* was published under his name alone, although Paula wrote some of the tales on her own. She preferred, however, to remain in the background as a "hidden person." The book which brought Martin Buber worldwide recognition, was dedicated to Paula in recognition of the "enormous impact" she had on him and on the writing of the book. In the form of a poem entitled "Do You Still Know It?" the dedication acknowledges the intimacy of their relationship and the impact Paula's Christianity was having on his thinking. The poem ends with the words "I and Thou," words which became the title of his major work. All real life is an encounter, or meeting, Buber believed, to which "a man must bring his whole being, his genuine self," whether he was Jewish or Christian. Paula could become a Jew and continue to believe in Christ; indeed, for Martin, she "brought Jesus into close relation with the mysteries of Jewish faith."

Paula was by no means merely an inspiration to her brilliant husband; she was a writer who manifested her own spirituality, creativity, and mysticism in many books and essays written under a pen name, Georg Munk. After her death, three of her books were published by her husband in one volume entitled *Spirits and Men.* In his introduction to this collection, Martin Buber says that the stories are not fairy tales, not romantic ghost stories, "but genuine tales of spirits, reports of them, of spirits which in a special kind of natural mystery enter into our lives and perhaps abandon themselves to them. In her writing images become events."

One day, a student, who introduced himself as "a Buber-person," asked his professor, "Dr. Buber, would it be correct to define a successful marriage, such as yours, as a marriage where there is love and work?" Professor Buber smiled: "I would say, love, work, faith, responsibility, and a great sense of humor." He was speaking from experience, for he and Paula had found that their marriage was not merely love and work.

In the midst of a busy life that included teaching at the university, writing books, raising a family, and dialoguing with friends, many of whom differed with them, Martin and Paula felt a dark part of life intruding. The year was 1933 and the Nazis had come to power in Germany. Evil "is not aware of the otherness of the other but instead tries to incorporate the other into himself." Thus at the University of Frankfurt, where Buber was teaching Judaism and comparative religion, he and Paula began to be in jeopardy.

Despite warnings and threats, Martin and Paula decided to continue to speak out, to remain true to their responsibility toward God and humanity, as they were remaining true to their responsibility toward each other, undertaken at their first meeting. Professor Ernst Simon, then the chairman of a committee working for a Jewish homeland, said, "Anyone who did not see Buber in the 1930s has not seen true civil courage." Neither Martin nor Paula were afraid to challenge Hitler's regime directly. However, by 1938 the situation in Germany had deteriorated to a point of no return, and Martin Buber was silenced by the Nazis.

The Bubers were urged to leave Germany, to come to Jerusalem, but they kept putting off the journey. Martin said that they wanted to travel to Palestine as tourists, not as immigrants, so that they could return to Germany if the German Jews needed them. But the pressure on them became too great and they finally left for Jerusalem, where Martin accepted the post of professor of philosophy at the Hebrew University. They were to spend the remaining twenty-seven years of their marriage with Jerusalem as their home base, and for almost all of that time, the house on Lovers of Zion Street was their home. Martin Buber's fame became worldwide, but he always acknowledged that Paula was "the touchstone of everything I have done."

After the fall of Hitler, Martin again lectured in Germany to enthusiastic audiences of students. Their life continued to be a life of "meeting" that included the great writers, religious, philosophers, artists, and musicians of the century. Among those they met were Jacques and Raissa Maritain—he the noted Christian philosopher and a convert to Catholicism, she his Jewish wife who converted with him. Jacques and Raissa shared an intimacy similar to that of Martin and Paula. In her journal (published by Jacques after her death), Raissa wrote, "But does there then remain nothing for heaven of the union of husband and wife, faithful to each other till death? What remains is what friendship may have created of purely spiritual union between them, of similarity of soul, of equality of merits, perhaps, in a life in which everything has been in common."

And everything in Paula and Martin's life had been in common. He wanted the world to know that whatever came to him came to her; whatever honor paid him was paid her. He wanted the world to know, but above all he wanted Paula to know. When it was written of him, "Because Martin Buber lived, there is more love in the world than there would have been without him," Martin would have added that without Paula there would not have been Martin. After his death *The New York Times* called Buber "a theological bridge-builder long before ecumenism achieved its present popularity"; Martin would have reminded the writer that Paula was one pillar of that bridge. Senator Abraham Ribicoff had read into the *Congressional Record,* "Martin Buber served as bridge-builder between Judaism and Christianity in an era that abounds with divisive forces"; Martin would have asked that Paula's name be read into the record too. Trappist monk Thomas Merton wrote, "Martin Buber contributed so much to Christian personalism"; Martin would have assured him that without Paula no contribution would have been possible.

Buber never wrote about his marriage itself in any of his major works, for his relationship with Paula was a deeply personal matter in which the "I" and the "Thou" were one. He also felt that one marriage cannot be a valid example for another marriage. "If my marriage is exemplary, it means that it shows me what openness and responsibility has been for *my* marriage," he told some of his students at the University of Heidelberg.

If Martin Buber experienced a lover's reserve in talking to others about his beloved, he showed no reticence in letting Paula know what she meant to him. He dedicated books to her, wrote poems to her (in her youth, her middle years, into her old age), and had her in mind whenever he spoke of marriage, even after her death. On his fiftieth birthday, thirty years before her death, he wrote the poem "On the Day of Looking Back," dedicated to her. He speaks of Paula as the iridescent spirit encompassing him:

> Then both spirit and world became open to me,
> The lies burst, and what was, was enough.
> You brought it about that I beheld,—
> Brought about? You only lived,
> You, element and woman,
> Soul and nature.[2]

In his seventies he dedicated one of his major works (*The Way Of Man*) with these words: "Responsibility is the navel-string of Creation—P.B." (P.B. is, of course, Paula Buber.)

Only a few months before his own death, Martin selected some essays, poems, letters, and reviews that he wanted in what was to be his last book, *A Believing Humanism: My Testament, 1902–1965.* All of his poems to Paula, all the dedications to her, and the introduction he wrote to her collected stories are included in this last testament that consisted of "that and only that which appears to me today as a valid expression, worthy of surviving, of an experience, a feeling, a decision, yes, even a dream."

The day after the serenade commemorating Martin Buber's eighty-fifth birthday, the house on Lovers of Zion Street was peaceful. The old man was in his study, the walls lined with over 40,000 books, the shelves displaying the many tokens of esteem, the many framed awards. His nine cats came in or went out through their own cat-door, paying no attention to the visitors, a young married couple who had been given permission by his granddaughter to visit, but "very briefly." Martin, though, insisted that they stay for tea and *Kekse.* Martin pointed to a "beautiful giant box" filled with cards and telegrams. "My granddaughter put it here to remind me to answer all the congratulations received on this milestone day of my life-way from men who on the way have met me bodily or spiritually." He looked at his guests and changed the subject by asking them about their life together. They, however, wanted to ask him about marriage, his marriage to Paula Buber. The young wife wanted to know how to recognize an exemplary marriage.

Martin Buber smiled. "I'll tell you a Hasidic story," he said. "A father took his son to see how a married couple were sitting together in a room with plain board walls. 'What impression did the two make on you?' the father asked. 'As we entered the room,' the son answered, 'they seemed to me like Adam and Eve before they sinned.' The father continued, 'And how did the room in which they were seated look to you?' 'Like Paradise,' the son said. 'That is just how it looked to me,' the father agreed."

Martin Buber finished the story and was silent.

7

Raissa and Jacques Maritain

The ancient halls of the University of Paris, the Sorbonne, with its courts and corridors, had for generations—since the Middle Ages—been the scene of romantic encounters. When nineteen-year-old Jacques Maritain and eighteen-year-old Raissa Oumansoff met there, it was love at first sight, in the eternal tradition of such places.

Love at first sight, Jane Austen said, is a sign of giddiness. But with Jacques and Raissa, love at first sight seems to have been a recognition of their mutual destiny. They saw each other's faces and knew each other.

Over half a century later, when Jacques Maritain published *Raissa's Journal* after her death, among the entries was this one:

> The gifts of God have infinite expansion. But they are at the same time for this or that individual. First, God made the child Jacques Maritain to be born on the 19th November 1882 in Paris. Ten months later he made the child Raissa Oumansoff be born on 12 September in Rostov-on-the-Don.[1]

How two such different people from such distant places could have been fated to come together is in itself mysteriously significant. Jacques was born into one of the chief liberal democratic families in France. His grandfather, a leader in French political life, was a member of the famous French Academy. Jacques' mother was a woman with "an indomitable spirit of liberty," whose passions were political but definitely not religious.

Raissa was a Jewish girl whose "maternal grandfather was a Hasid. . . ."[2] (The Hasidic Jews, as is well known today, thanks to Martin Buber and Chaim Potok, were religious to the point of being "ecstatics.") Raissa was an exceptionally bright child; she was admitted to the Russian lycée on the basis of her intelligence. But her parents decided to leave Russia because of the quota imposed by the Russian schools on the admission of Jewish children. They wanted to live in a country that would never bar their children from good schools. Because France had no such quotas, they moved to Paris with their two small daughters.

When Raissa was thirteen, her father gave her the works of Victor Hugo. "I moved a step forward in the knowledge of mankind by reading *Les Miserables,* my first novel. I was passionately excited by reading this book; it put me in close communication with beings created by a poet."[3] But it also opened her to a world she had not known, the world of awful poverty and harsh injustice.

"I wondered if God really existed. . . . I reasoned thus: If God exists, He is infinitely good and all powerful. But if He is good how can He permit suffering? And if He is all powerful how can He tolerate the wicked? Therefore He is not all powerful nor infinitely good; therefore He does not exist."[4]

In another part of the same city, another child, the boy Jacques, was undergoing similar questionings. It was an era of triumphant scientism. Intelligent people expressed opinions that took for granted that science had answered all the questions that religion had left unanswered—all mysteries were solved.

At seventeen Raissa entered the Sorbonne, taking courses in the sciences. In response to her questions about the mystery of life, her professors would smile and inevitably tell her not to bother with such thoughts. "That is mysticism," they chided.

One day, as she came out of her plant physiology class, a young man came up to her. Raissa wrote of their first meeting in her book, *We Have Been Friends Together.* ". . . I saw coming toward me a young man with a gentle face, a heavy shock of blond hair, a light beard and slightly stoop-shouldered carriage. He introduced himself and said he was forming a committee of students to start a movement of protest among French writers and university people against the ill-treatment to which Russian Socialist students had been subject in their own country. (At that time in Russia there were student riots which were severely repressed by the Czarist police.) And he asked me to join this committee. Such was my first meeting with Jacques Maritain."[5]

He, too, wrote about her. He had noticed her because she was always alone and seemed much younger than the other students. He had noted her slender grace, her "marvellous smile" and "the extraordinary light of her wonderful eyes." They became inseparable, walking and talking, discussing with the passion of young people the ultimate questions of life, politics, religion, and the meaning of it all, if any. They sometimes walked for miles, forgetting to go home, not turning up for meals, and causing both sets of parents to worry. Raissa wrote, "Did anything else exist in comparison with all we had to tell each other? Together we had to think out the entire universe anew, the meaning of life, the fate of man, the justice and injustice of societies."[6]

Sometimes they disagreed, and when they did, it was unbearable; they would keep seeking to understand each other better. "Disagreement was intolerable to us . . . in order to be reconciled there was nothing for it but to try to understand each other and to solve the problem."

One summer afternoon they were walking in the Jardin des Plantes, a park on the Left Bank of the Seine. They spoke of all the young people of their generation who were committing suicide. "In Austria, in Germany, in Italy, in France, thousands of suicides . . . due to this despair." Raissa said passionately that a life without meaning was worse than death. Jacques countered with the thought that one could live at least in order to do good, to fight for justice and human rights, but Raissa eloquently insisted that, "If we must give up the hope of finding any meaning whatever for the word Truth, for the distinction of good and evil, of just from unjust, it is no longer possible to live humanly."[7] She did not mind a sad life, but an absurd life could not be endured.

"Before leaving the Jardin des Plantes we reached a solemn decision . . . we would extend credit to existence, look upon it as an experiment to be made, in the hope that the meaning of life would reveal itself. But if the experiment should not be successful, the solution would be suicide."[8]

But when they told their friend Charles Péguy about their decision, he assured them that he had found a philosopher who would convince them that life did indeed have meaning, and that behind all temporal things was a moving spirit, a spirit of life, an *élan vital!* He lectured at the Collège de France, across the street from the Sorbonne, and his name was Henri Bergson. The Collège de France was looked down on by the Sorbonne, and so was Henri Bergson, because he refused to run with the pack and follow the materialism and scientism of the era. After hearing Bergson, both Jacques and Raissa realized how much there was to learn from him and from the great mystics like Plotinus whom Bergson introduced. When summer vacation came, Raissa began to read Plotinus with deep interest. One day, sitting on her bed, she read a passage in which Plotinus spoke of the soul's loving encounter with God, the mysterious union of love. "The next moment I was on my knees before the book, covering the page I had just read with passionate kisses, and my heart burning with love."[9]

It was a prophetic moment—her first conscious experience of a power, an energy, connected to prayer. When Jacques came to see her, she recounted her experience, and they spoke of the possibility of experiencing Infinity without losing their finite human love for each other. He was sitting on the rug beside her chair and she put her hand on his head. He reached up, took her hand, and kissed it, and at that moment they promised to love each other forever. Since they were still in school, they agreed to keep their betrothal a secret.

Two years went by, and in the summer of 1904, Raissa became ill. She had contracted an infection from drinking polluted water while on a vacation with her family and Jacques. An abscess in her throat grew so large that it was strangling her. Jacques held her, whispering, "Breathe, breathe." Meanwhile Vera, her younger sister, got on the train to Paris, returning that same evening with a surgeon. He said that he had to operate at once. While Vera held the lamp and Jacques held Raissa's head, the doctor removed the retropharyngeal abscess. He said that it was not a moment too soon. A few more hours and she would have died.

After that experience, Jacques insisted they must marry as soon as she was strong enough. A few months later, in the fall, they were wed, and moved into an apartment near the university. Jacques went on with his courses, but Raissa—not yet strong enough to go back to the university—kept house and went to Bergson's lectures. One day she came upon a book entitled *La Femme Pauvre* written by Léon Bloy, an eccentric, radical Catholic. This book changed their lives.

"What struck us forcibly on first reading *La Femme Pauvre* was the immensity of this believer's soul, his burning zeal for justice, the beauty of a lofty doctrine which for the first time rose up before our eyes."[10] They learned that the author had repudiated money and fame "through the love for a God Who took on poverty for our sakes." Filled with respect for Léon Bloy, this pilgrim of the Absolute, as he called himself, they wrote him an admiring letter and "very timidly" sent him a little money. They were both very poor themselves, but Bloy was destitute. He replied with a gift of his books and an invitation to visit him.

Years later, Jacques Maritain wrote, "June 25, 1905, two children of twenty mounted the sempiternal stairway which leads up to Sacré-Coeur. They carried in themselves that distress which is the only serious product of modern culture, and a sort of active despair lightened only (they did not know why) by the inner assurance that the Truth for which they hungered, and without which it was almost impossible for them to accept life, would one day be shown to them."[11]

When they entered the humble house, its walls covered with pictures and books, they were met by Madame Léon Bloy and their two small daughters, Véronique and Madeleine. "Léon Bloy seemed almost timid, he spoke but little and very low."

Yet they did not feel like strangers in that house. Bloy and his wife simply adopted them. "Once the threshold of that house was crossed, all values were dislocated, as though by an invisible switch. One knew or one guessed, that only one sorrow existed there—not to be a saint."[12]

Their visits to the Bloys became frequent. They felt enfolded in love, and went often to share their poverty. Léon Bloy's ideas freed Jacques and Raissa from the fear of religion, and his teachings influenced them profoundly. Much later, Jacques and Raissa were to affect the Church as they had been affected by Léon Bloy. When Hitler came into power, Pope Pius XI, influenced by the Old Testament approach of Maritain, issued his famous statement exhorting Christians to cease and desist from all anti-Semitism: "By Christ and in Christ, we are the spiritual descendants of Abraham. No, it is not possible for Christians to have any part in anti-Semitism. . . . Spiritually we are Semites."[13]

But long before they became influential, the young lovers were still finding their way to the scriptures. They were ignorant of Judaism and of Christianity. Their reading had given wide berth to religion and scripture. Bloy did not try to convert them, but simply put into their hands not apologetics, not arguments proving the truth of the Church or of Christianity, but only the lives of the great mystics and saints, such as Teresa of Avila.

Now Jacques and Raissa felt drawn to visit churches. One day, after visiting the Cathedral of Chartres, they were returning home. Raissa, by the car window, watched the forest glide by. Suddenly the feeling of God overwhelmed her with a sense of Presence. "I was looking out of the window and thinking of nothing in particular. Suddenly a great change took place in me, as if from the perception of the senses, I had passed over to an entirely inward perception. . . . The whole forest seemed to be speaking and to speak of Another—seemed to have no other function than to *signify* the Creator."[14] She and Jacques spoke of these experiences, and he later wrote in one of his books, "At the sight of something or other a soul will know in an instant that these things do not exist through themselves and that God is."[15]

Raissa's thoughts were like the rungs by which Jacques climbed his own ladder of thoughts, thoughts he incorporated into books that became famous in the first half of the twentieth century. After Raissa's death, Jacques wrote, "If there is anything good in my philosophical work, and in my books, this has its deep source and light in her contemplative prayer and in the oblation of herself she made to God."[16]

Jacques's fascination with Raissa's thoughts endured throughout their marriage. One of Raissa's *Journal* notes, dated May 1944 (the couple were in their sixties then), relates a remark to one of their many godchildren: "There is no book in the world one does not have the right to question except the scriptures—but the scriptures one doesn't understand." Jacques was so delighted with this remark that he wrote it down "and stuck it up on the drawing room wall (from which, of course, I removed it)."[17]

Eventually Jacques and Raissa decided to become Catholic converts, and when they did, Raissa's sister Vera joined them. Jacques later wrote what conversion to a specific church meant: "Religion is essentially that which no philosophy can be; a relation of person to person with all the risk, the mystery, the dread, the confidence, the delight, and the torment that lie in such a relationship . . . one enters oneself with all one's baggage—one's own existence and flesh and blood—into the vital relationship. . . ."[18] By situating their marriage-love within the fire of God-love, Jacques and Raissa did not then realize that they were taking up a life together in the heart of a fiery furnace!

Everyone—not just their parents, who soon accepted the inevitable—was shocked by the couple's conversion. Many friends dropped away. "The solitude our conversion had created about us did not surprise us. . . . Jacques broke with most of his acquaintances of the Sorbonne."[19] He could not get a teaching post in the antireligious climate of the universities, so he took a job compiling a dictionary for a small publisher and began writing articles on philosophy—inspired by Bergson, and by his Catholic conversion. It was soon apparent that he had a gift for writing about philosophical and theological subjects and that he was original. He discussed a realm of ideas that had been shut off for centuries in the Church and in the universities.

Meanwhile, Raissa discovered more fascinating books to share with her husband—the works of Saint Thomas Aquinas. Aquinas was to become Maritain's great work, for he made the structure of this great thinker's mind accessible to modern times. After Raissa's death, a friend wrote to Jacques, "She was collaborating with you all the time. Nothing of your abundant work has been published by you without her having followed it at different stages of development right up to the final version; and you attached a peerless value to her vigilant and penetrating judgment."[20]

Jacques himself wrote, "She sacrificed everything . . . in spite of all her suffering, and, at certain moments of an almost total exhaustion . . . and because the collaboration I had always asked of her was, for her, a sacred duty . . . revising in manuscript everything I have written. . . ."[21] Fortunately, all during their marriage Raissa's sister Vera lived with the couple. Utterly devoted, she liked to do all the things Raissa found difficult—shopping, marketing, and running the household.

Almost from the moment Jacques and Raissa became converts, they lost their right to be alone together and found themselves at the center of a human commotion. Much as they might have longed for a hermitage, they were not given this grace but had to live in two worlds at once. "If God does not call one to solitude, one must live with God in the multitude,"[22] wrote Raissa. "A spiritual destiny is a light bridge thrown across the abyss, or the peak of a rock rising above the ocean."[23] The soul has a sudden view that makes her dizzy, "because she is *separated* but not yet *withdrawn* from the world. . . . Anyone who has not the experience of this 'separation' does not know, either, the road on which he is treading; he does not know the distinction between the two worlds."[24]

The awareness that this couple lived both in and out of the world was what fascinated people and drew them to the Maritains, for many sought to enter the same experiences. Jacques, meanwhile, had become very famous, constantly in demand as a lecturer. Because Raissa's health often would not permit her to travel with him, they endured separations that both found difficult. The letters they wrote to each other over the years, when separated, belong to the great love letters of the ages. Jacques would tell her how painful the separation was and speak of his anxiety over her.

"Go on loving me like this," she replied in one of her letters, "I need a great deal of love in order to live. . . . What a terrible vocation!" She referred to her own vocation, the call to mystical prayer. "It is for that God has placed your marvellous love at my side. For with whom would I have been able to live such a vocation, except with you? . . . What is wonderful is that I can take rest in your heart without in any way hindering God's action in us. God is so much with you and you are truly my only sweetness in this world."[25]

Raissa, a complete introvert, never could adapt to being publicly religious. It was easier for Jacques, who came from a long line of politically public-minded people. But neither of them relished having their spiritual life "on display." As young converts, they had imagined they could be quietly baptized by Léon Bloy, and then live a simple spiritual life that was their own secret. Bloy told a friend, "In their ignorance they thought that I could baptize them myself. . . . I had to explain to them that since they were not in danger of death and since it was easy to obtain a priest, they must receive baptism as it is conferred by the Church and not the simple rite administered *in extremis* by a person."[26]

Raissa wrote, "We thought in very truth that all this could be a matter between ourselves and God and our godfather. We dreaded all externalization." But the Maritains became a "school." Centers sprang up called "Maritain Centers," where people came to study the thought of Thomas Aquinas and to discuss religion and Catholicism and Judaism. No matter how many people came, Raissa and Jacques welcomed them into "the family." Their friends, most of whom were artists, writers, and philosophers who knew how valuable and precious time was to the creative person, marveled at the "supreme self-discipline" which enabled these two people to be constantly open to all who came. Each visitor was treated as a person sent by God, "and each one came back from there, moved to the depths of soul" (wrote one who was a constant visitor), "by having been *accepted* and recognized personally . . . this ability to listen, to understand others without ever forcing their confidence, demanded, particularly of Raissa, the hostess and the heart of the home, a truly prodigal self-giving and self-effacement. . . ."[27]

Their marriage was not easy; nothing was easy, for they were pitched and tossed in the waves of life. As Jacques became more famous, resentment and controversy often surrounded him. For example, the Maritains took a position on the Spanish Civil War opposed to a great many of their fellow Catholics, who supported Franco. When in February of 1937, Jacques signed, with other prominent Frenchmen, a protest against the bombing of Madrid, and the strafing by German planes of the town of Guernica, he was reviled and denounced as a "liberal" and a "communist." Because he had become such a famous Catholic and had influenced Catholic thought toward openness and intellectual awareness, he was plotted against by those who were archconservative. In her *Journal,* Raissa wrote that they received several letters during this period of their lives, "warning Jacques of what is being hatched against him in Rome. They want to catch him in fault; Franco's partisans haven't disarmed. Now they want to convict Jacques of error on the question of implicit faith. It will be done in an article by Father Cordovani in the *Osservatore,* where he will not be named but clearly identifiable. Misery! During this time Father Coughlin can talk every day to thousands of Catholics as a nazi, a racist, an anti-Semite, without incurring any penalty. . . ."[28] The Church was angrily divided between right and left. The Spanish Civil War dramatized the divisions among the peoples of the Western world. It was a prelude to World War II.

In January, 1940, the Maritains left France because Jacques was asked to teach a course at the Institute of Medieval Studies in Toronto, Canada, and then go on to lecture at several universities in the United States. They were in New York when the fall of France came six months later. In June, 1940, the Germans crushed the French armies and were moving toward Paris. Jacques and Raissa loved France in a deeply personal way. On that June day, as they listened to the news on the radio, Raissa and Vera, her sister, sat on the sofa, weeping. Jacques was pacing back and forth in despair. It was one of the harshest trials of their life.

It was providential, wrote Julie Kernan, that Jacques had brought with him his wife and sister-in-law, for Raissa and Vera were Jews; they would all have been in gravest danger.

The Maritains would have preferred not to be drawn into political action, but their marriage was based on a dramatic spiritual belief that compelled them as forcefully into the center of the political arena as into the center of religious turmoil. Other marriages could rest securely on a basis of the human family's need for a sanctuary against the outside world of troubles. Theirs was different. Everybody's marriage is different, noted Raissa, when asked why their marriage was so successful.

"There is a clumsy insistence on the psychology of married people . . . married people make their own psychology. It is dangerous to give as essential properties of marriage ones which only belong to marriage fulfilled in exceptional conditions of love. . . ." As for those who insisted on giving marriage advice, especially priests, she declared forthrightly, "When one sees the number of celibate analysts who devote themselves to the problem of marriage, one has the feeling that it is the analysts most of all who would need to get married,"[29] Raissa wrote in her *Journal*.

The Maritains' marriage was indeed fulfilled in exceptional conditions of love. When they had been married barely ten years and were in their early thirties, they went to kneel in the Cathedral of Versailles to take a vow of celibacy. No one knew until after Raissa died; then Jacques revealed the secret. "It was after taking long counsel with Father Clerissac . . . we decided to renounce a thing which marriage fulfills, a deep need of the human being—both of body and spirit. . . . I do not say that any such decision was easy to take. . . . It implied no scorn for nature but a desire to follow at any price at least one of the counsels of the perfect life." He also said, "One of the great graces of our life was that . . . our mutual love was infinitely increased."[30]

The couple needed all the grace of their strengthened mutual love for the political horrors that the times were unfolding. They, who had tried to keep clear of political actions, were discovering what the new age was discovering, what Gandhi had spoken of when he said, "I am told that religion and politics are different spheres of life. But I would say without a moment's hesitation and yet in all modesty that those who claim this do not know what religion is."[31]

Raissa wrote in her *Journal* that their souls were choked with the dust and ashes of the Nazi furnaces. "Human madness and human cruelty have been given permission to go to all lengths . . . of the six million massacred we counted very close friends . . . when one can put a name to a few of those who died in Auschwitz, in Belsen, or in Dachau, and call up a face among them, the vast sorrow one feels for all the other victims itself assumes a face which haunts you."[32]

As always, the Maritains were beseiged by those who saw in them a symbol of belief in the good, the true, and the beautiful, when, wherever one turned, there appeared only the bad, the false, and the ugly. "While the swastika was triumphing in Europe," wrote Jacques, "we had all the same to keep up our spirits and those of others." Friends were comforted when they came to the Maritains—Jacques wrote that they were especially affected by "the light and kind of winged gaiety that emanated from Raissa."

On New Year's Eve of 1943, a group had gathered to be with them. On the stroke of twelve, Marc Chagall arrived with his wife Bella and their daughter. He was carrying a great bouquet of red roses for Raissa.

When the war finally ended, General de Gaulle, who had become head of the French government, asked Jacques Maritain to accept the post of French ambassador to the Holy See. De Gaulle also asked that the Vatican replace the ultraconservative papal nuncio in Paris, who had helped foment bitter divisions within the Church. "The Vatican replaced him by a little-known apostolic delegate . . . Archbishop Angelo Roncalli, later to be Good Pope John."

Although Jacques feared that Raissa's health might not be up to all the social duties, she insisted that he accept the post, and she undertook her own duties with a will. "Raissa filled her role as ambassadress with such grace and charm that everyone was impressed,"[33] wrote a friend. The Pope's deputy secretary of state, Monsignor Montini, was much influenced by them. Later, when he was Pope Paul VI, he would refer to Jacques Maritain as "my teacher."

After three years of service, Jacques Maritain asked to be freed from his duty, and he and Raissa and Vera returned to Princeton, where he had been offered a resident professorship. A few years later he was struck down by a coronary thrombosis, but Raissa and Vera cared for him day and night, determined that he should not die. He recovered, but shortly afterward Vera, seemingly the strong one, succumbed to cancer. Raissa and Jacques nursed her with the same unremitting faithfulness, refusing to put her in a hospital. She died on the last day of 1959 and was buried at Princeton.

Sad and exhausted, they decided to go home to France. Six months after Vera's death, they arrived in Paris, on July 7, 1960. As they entered their hotel room, Raissa fell down. It was a cerebral thrombosis. "Four agonising months, Raissa was walled up in herself," wrote Jacques Maritain later in his Foreword to *Raissa's Journal*. "In the supreme battle in which she was engaged, no one here on earth could help her, myself no more than anyone else." He described her full lucidity, humor, concern for others, "and the extraordinary light of her wonderful eyes."[34]

After her death, the solitude and prayer they had both dreamed of was given Jacques Maritain. He went to live with the Little Brothers at Toulouse. "I am the father of sixty devoted sons,"[35] he reported to friends. He went on writing, teaching, living the monastic life. At the age of eighty he took vows as a religious brother.

On his desk he kept two pictures of Raissa and each day collected fresh flowers to put before them. Before he died he went back to the Jardin des Plantes. It was January 1973 when he took the journey one last time "to the exact spot where he and Raissa had met during their student days when they were trying to decide whether or not life was worth living. A photographer wished to take his picture, and this was the last picture of Jacques Maritain, taken on the exact spot where he and Raissa made their famous pact of a death by suicide or a life utterly committed to ultimate and absolute meaning."[36]

Four months later, at the age of 91, he died of a heart attack. "In a simple wooden coffin his body was set before the altar . . . so many people wished to attend the funeral services, they had to hold it outdoors at an improvised altar." The coffin was carried by the Little Brothers to the cemetery and Jacques was laid beside Raissa.

In her book about their life and times (*We Have Been Friends Together*), written while they were exiles during World War II and the Holocaust, Raissa wrote that their epoch was one of "great spiritual renewal at the brink of the decline of a world . . . those who did not know these times cannot imagine what they were. But their abundant seed will later bear fruit in a form which we ourselves cannot imagine." Their marriage was part of the work of seedtime.

8

Nadezhda and Osip Mandelstam

Nothing is more destructive to the family circle than wars and revolution. The center does not hold. This truth is vividly recorded in the twentieth-century writings of Soviet Russia. But at the same time stories of war and revolution often reveal the tenacity with which certain gifted pairs of lovers literally hold the center together with their lives. They go to their deaths for love, for poetry, and for the imagination, that extraordinary gift of the Creator.

"Imagination," wrote Thomas Merton, "is a discovering faculty ... the imagination is something which enables us to discover unique present meaning in a given moment of our life."[1]

The Nobel prize novelists of Russia, Boris Pasternak and Alexander Solzhenitsyn, wrote all their works on this great theme. In his novel *The First Circle,* Solzhenitsyn narrates the story of prisoners who risk their lives, secretly passing from hand to hand a forbidden book. It is not a political tract; it is a volume of poems.

"I do not know how it is elsewhere, but here, in this country, poetry is a healing, life-giving thing, and people have not lost the gift of being able to drink of its inner strength. People can be killed for poetry here—a sign of unparalleled respect—because they are still capable of living by it,"[2] wrote Nadezhda Mandelstam. Her husband had been considered one of the foremost of modern Russian poets. Unlike Pasternak and Solzhenitsyn, he did not survive his imprisonment for having so dangerous a creative gift. As a woman who was determined to hold the center, Nadezhda had but one purpose after Osip's death, to save his poetry. She committed to memory the vast bulk of his poems. She would later write, ironically but also longingly: "To think we could have had an ordinary family life with its bickerings, broken hearts and divorce suits."[3]

Nadezhda was born into an affluent Jewish family just as the twentieth century began. Eight years older than Nadezhda, Osip spent his childhood in St. Petersburg, though he had been born in Warsaw. He was educated at the Sorbonne and his first volume of poetry was published when he was twenty-three.

Nadezhda and Osip met in the Junk Shop—a meeting place of poets and artists. The couple's mutual attraction was instantaneous and was noticed by everyone. Nadezhda was just twenty, but small, and looked much younger, more like a girl in her teens. Osip was barely thirty, but looked older. Everyone told her he was too old for her, including the writer Ilya Ehrenburg, who took her for a long walk through the streets and tried to persuade her that Osip was not for her; he was too old and unreliable. It was no use. She and Osip went a few days later to a Greek coffee shop and got married "by one who came from a priest's family." The place was Kiev, Russia, and the date was 1919. They considered this unorthodox ceremony a marriage sacrament.

Three years later when the Mandelstams wanted to get on a train from Kiev to Moscow, the commandant of the train refused them a berth until they could prove they were married. They went at once and got a certificate of marriage from the Registrar's Office in Kiev. So they had both a sacramental marriage and a legal ritual. The sacrament, performed by "one descended from a priest's family," was sealed with a ring. ("The day before we had married, we bought ourselves a couple of blue rings for a kopeck apiece near Mikhailov monastery.")[4]

Nadezhda found that living with this poet was a strange experience, like living with something not yet tamed, a bit wild. "There was something chaste, in the true sense of the word . . . but such a thing was beyond the wildest imagination of the people around us.

Innocence of mind or body, or any other kind, if they had ever encountered it, would have seemed to them like a sprained limb or broken bone."[5]

Both of them had a quality of innocence, wandering like Adam and Eve, after the Fall, among the ruins. The cities of Russia were in ruins and, like multitudes of others, the Mandelstams moved from place to place, homeless. If they found an abandoned apartment, they moved in.

"One day we looked out of the window and saw a cart piled with naked corpses . . . another day we saw a crazed mob running down some red-haired women and literally tearing them limb from limb."[6]

In one place where they lived, the room had no door; it had been chopped up for firewood. Osip wrote a comic poem: "What Street is this? / This is Mandelstam Street."

But they both knew that there would never be a street named after him in Russia. Nadezhda only hoped for a grave that was not nameless. "There is no grave on which to put a cross, and in this country we call our own, they have for many years been trying to stamp out all he did,"[7] she later wrote.

When Osip was seventeen and attending the Sorbonne in France, he wrote a letter to a friend expressing nostalgia for the comforts of a stable, middle-class life.

> I have strange tastes; I love the patches of reflected electric light on the surface of Lake Leman, respectful lackeys, the silent flight of the elevator, the marble vestibule of the hotel and the English-women who play Mozart with two or three official listeners in the half-darkened salon. I love bourgeois, European comfort and am devoted to it not only physically but emotionally.[8]

Undoubtedly Osip had some forebodings, for none of the comforts and charms of middle-class life were ever to be his and Nadezhda's. Society was in an upheaval, and all its structures were crashing. They had to keep on the move just to get out of the way of falling timbers and flaming debris.

As a boy Osip Mandelstam had written, "If in this life there is no sense, then to talk of life makes no sense." But he and Nadezhda dauntlessly insisted on making sense of their lives, at least in their union. But simply to stay together was an enormous task. People who got separated from each other rarely met again, for communication systems were in a state of chaos.

Osip and Nadezhda nearly lost each other right after they had agreed never to be separated. Osip had gone for a visit to the Crimea. Nadezhda had remained in Kiev living with her parents, where Osip would be able to find her. But on the day he came back and went to their address, they had gone; they had been evicted. It was only by chance that Nadezhda returned to get something from the empty apartment, and at that moment Osip entered; they were reunited. He read her all the poems he had written and said they would never go anywhere alone again. From then until the night of May 1, 1938, they were inseparable. "He sensed how few our days together were fated to be."

Osip had an inner strength that continually surprised Nadezhda: "His free acceptance of his lot and boundless gratitude for all he had been granted; the sky, the air, the grass, breathing, love—these were the treasures in his possession."[9] Though he dared not cultivate illusions of future success and good fortune, he wrote a poem saying that he valued his "living allotment of air."

Nadezhda (Nadia) did not feel restricted by his intense possessiveness, though she was aware that he meant to shape her, as if he could make her exactly the partner he wished her to be. "He treats you like a puppy," one of the writers told her angrily. "Those were the years when all Osip's efforts were directed to isolating me from other people, making me his own, breaking me in and adapting me to himself. Those were the years in which he stubbornly trained me not to read but to listen to poetry, to learn to appreciate it by ear,"[10] Nadezhda wrote.

He wouldn't let her hold a book in her hand. She had to develop the ear and the memory for the work that was to be her only center of meaning, in time to come. "I felt like a horse in the hands of a trainer. . . . He was lucky in that I was a willing learner and very easy to manage."

The sophisticated, liberated, intellectual Russian-Jewish girl was in some respects very like the simple, humble, intuitive English girl, Catherine Blake—they were women who seemed free from any insecurity about their own spiritual freedom! Perhaps they were aware that, subtly, *they* were the animal trainers, snaring the elusive unicorns. Nadia did not worry about what others said of her behavior. When Osip called, she came running. "I can still see myself in my mind's eye running along after him over the sunlit grounds in front of the building and then at his side up a steep lane . . . I was wearing high-heeled shoes with soles almost worn through . . . M. was walking quickly with great strides, I had to run, skipping along beside him . . . he went on at me a long time about how he had spent a whole hour trying to find me, about how hard I was making it for him to do his work! Nonsense, I said, you took only five minutes to find me, and you must stop treating me like a puppy—it's making us a laughingstock."[11]

For a time Osip and Nadia lived in Moscow, then went on to Leningrad. By chance they found a beautiful apartment that had been vacated by owners who had fled the country. Everyone wanted to move in with them. One day Osip brought home a young woman whom he had run into on the street. Her name was Olga, and he had known her when she was a little girl. As soon as she saw the apartment she determined to take Osip away from Nadezhda. "She came every day, vamping M. under my very nose," wrote Nadia. He would read Olga his poetry and go out with her and leave Nadezhda home. "At first I just didn't know what to think . . . only yesterday he couldn't live without me!" Lack of housing seemed to be an instrument of the devil.

Osip acted as if he were hypnotized. "She had her charms as even I, the injured party, was bound to admit: she was just a girl, still beautiful, helpless, defenseless, and lost in the city's terrible wilderness. Her husband had left her, and she and her son were totally dependent on her mother." And here was a beautiful apartment with enough space for all of them, as Olga's mother pointed out, attempting to persuade Osip to leave Nadia. "He must save Olga," her mother said, talking in front of Nadezhda, hoping that this would make her see that *she* must be the one to go. As for Osip, "he had a strange faraway expression. . . ." Perhaps he was testing her.

Nadezhda would have left with dignity, but she did not know where to go, for the housing shortage was overwhelming. Fortunately she remembered a friend. He had been in love with her for years. She sent him a message to come for her, packed her suitcase and wrote a farewell note to Osip, saying she would never come back, and left it on the table. But while she was waiting for her friend to arrive, Osip walked in, and as soon as he saw her suitcase, flew into a rage. When her friend came, Osip showed him out with the words: "Nadia is staying with me." Her friend went sadly away, shaking his head. Then Osip asked Nadezhda to get Olga on the phone for him. "He wanted to break with her in my hearing so I should have no doubt of it. He said goodbye to Olga very brusquely: 'I'm not coming, I'm staying with Nadia, you and I shall never see each other again, never! I don't like the way you treat people!' " But this incident had nearly destroyed their reality.

After that Osip and Nadia had a new understanding. "We became a real couple. Perhaps this was because we talked about our relationship for the first time and somehow realized what it was all about."[12] They agreed that freedom did not, or ought not to mean breaking up friendships, or smashing the fidelity of lovers. When she wrote her memoirs, Nadezhda Mandelstam said, "I think that my generation was wrong about the insignificance of family life, and I remember a crazy woman once came to see Ilya Ehrenburg, stood in the doorway, and shouted: 'Give me back my family life!' He could not get rid of her. I feel very much the same way. . . ."[13]

The Mandelstams went to live in Tsarskoya Selo, and Osip was permitted to write, as a literary critic, essays on literature for a while. At this time he wrote several works now regarded as classics, among them "Conversation with Dante," in which he wrote of visiting Italy: "Here is that immovable land and with it / I drink the cold mountain air of Christianity." He defined poetry as "play," in the playfulness of God: "Thanks to the wonderful bounty of Christianity, the whole of our two-thousand-year-old culture is setting the world free for play, for spiritual pleasure, for free imitation of Christ . . . joyful communion with God, a game that the Children play with their Father."[14]

One of the surprising compensations for the couple's hazardous existence was their ability to take life as a gamble. Osip was the one who taught Nadia this; the worse things got, the more lighthearted and cheerful he became. She was not able to take their fears and the threats against them as lightly. "It began to seem to me that I was the older . . . aged from fear."

By 1934 they were back in Moscow. Osip had written a poem

called *Journey to Armenia,* which contained icy criticisms of Stalin. He was told to disavow the book. Nadezhda went to the State Publishing House to argue on his behalf, but she was warned that he must disavow *Journey to Armenia,* or never see publication again. Late one night, Osip woke her up to tell her that he could not sleep, for he knew "that every poem was now written as though death were coming tomorrow." Nadia would gladly have pressed Osip to make a retraction, anything to save him, but she knew it would do no good. "Far from getting him to repent, I would only have brought a flood of mockery down on my head."

There was famine in the Ukraine, and the starving refugees, fleeing the land, crowded into train stations, dying by the hundreds. Osip wrote a poem about Stalin, describing his "cockroach whiskers" and "his fingers fat as grubs." He wrote of the "fawning half-men" who carried out Stalin's orders, and cursed him as a "Murderer and peasant-slayer."[15] Though the poem only circulated underground, Osip was arrested. The intervention of his friend Nikolai Bukharin, a fellow writer, at that time a Party member who was highly placed, saved him from death in Lubianka Prison. With reckless courage Pasternak came of his own free will to volunteer help. Few of the other writers whose spirits were with Osip Mandelstam were so daring.

The sentence was exile for three years. Nadezhda was given the generous permission to go with him—again, thanks to the intervention of a high official. Osip was permitted to go into exile in the city to which other poets and writers were sent, Voronezh. There the couple lived out the three-year term. He got work in the theatre and sometimes on newspapers and they were able to survive. After their exile they returned to Moscow, but were ordered to live outside the city, "in accordance with regulations for convicted persons." A few friends tried to arrange for help from the Union of Writers, but its members were cowed, and only anxious to follow the guidelines of the authorities of the State. Most friends were busy denouncing each other. But a few literary friends risked themselves. They were able to arrange for the Mandelstams to go to a rest home maintained by the Literary Fund, two hundred kilometers east of Moscow.

As soon as they arrived, Osip Mandelstam was arrested. "On the very night it happened, he tried to explain to me that something was becoming clearer to him, that he could see something he had not understood before." Exhausted from the journey, she fell asleep, still hearing his voice: "I think I've understood something . . . but you and I . . ." She had a terrible nightmare, woke up screaming and heard the knock on the door. "I was so horror-struck that we did not even say goodbye properly."[16]

It was May 1, 1938. She never saw her friend and lover—her husband—again. Osip had put his manuscripts in a wicker basket that had belonged to his mother, where he kept her letters to him. The first thing Nadezhda did, upon his arrest, was get back to Moscow to pick up the basket full of his manuscripts. The police were already out with a warrant to pick her up. She barely got away, and went to live in a small town outside of Moscow. There she got a job, working the night shift in a textile factory. In the daytime she went into Moscow to take her place in line with the hundreds of other women seeking to hand over a package or a food parcel, and trying to get information from the officials. She would trudge from one Moscow jail to another. "The guard behind the window at which we asked for information would snarl something and slam down the wooden shutter."

She wrote of those times. "A woman whose husband has been arrested (unless she herself was responsible for it) chases frantically selling off her possessions in order to raise enough money for food packages. I went the rounds desperately trying to sell books . . . at night I lay awake repeating M.'s poems. . . ."[17]

In 1939 she learned, indirectly, that the treatment of Osip Mandelstam had come up at a Central Committee meeting, and had been pointed to as an example of "excesses." She knew that he must be dead. In June 1940 she was issued a death certificate, which gave the date of his death as Christmas 1938.

Nadezhda envied war widows, who at least received some kind of memento. For her, there would never be any knowledge of how he had died. "The mass graves into which the bodies with tags on their legs were thrown are inaccessible. As a widow who was unable to bury her husband, I pay my respects to a body with a tag on its leg, remembering and mourning without tears, because we belong to a tearless generation."[18] She understood and envied the Greek heroine in the drama of *Antigone*. At least Antigone had been able to steal out at night and bury her dead brother.

A few years later—in 1942—she received a visit from a stranger. It was a man who had been imprisoned in the same camp where her husband had died. She learned then that he had died of typhus, from the cold, in a transit camp near Vladivostok, while awaiting transfer to a forced labor camp. His body was thrown in a trench with others—no one knew where.

The ex-prisoner remembered him well, because the poet was the only one of all the political prisoners whom the hardened criminals permitted into their loft. These rough men had committed crimes of violence, and looked down on "the politicals" as unworthy of associating with "true criminals." But like so many Russians of that first half of the century, they had a passion for poetry. Nadezhda's visitor described the scene to her: "The loft was lit by a candle— the poet sat with the criminals." He described the poet's gray stubble of beard and the yellow leather coat he was wearing, trying to keep warm, but shivering because it was a cold coat, made of yellow doghide and now in tatters, so that he had to hold the tatters together. "The criminals would save their crusts of bread to share with him, offering him bread for a poem. They listened in respectful silence and then would ask him to repeat the poem."

Now Nadezhda wandered alone, from one place to another, sometimes getting work as a teacher at a local school. But her central concern was to save her husband's work, "not to allow *them* to stamp out all traces of the man." She characterized this second period of her life as being: "in the tomb, which is exactly what it felt like . . . an unbelievable charnelhouse existence which dragged on for fifteen years—just waiting." What was she waiting for? She could not give up the confused and impossible need to find him, somewhere, somehow, to preserve memory: "We answer for everything—for every deed and every word—and memory invites us to consider why we have lived."

Nadezhda searched for a reason to go on living. Their lives had been sundered in two, and everything around her was inexplicable. "Instead of living my life, all I did was wait until its two severed parts could be joined together again. In such periods of waiting an aim in life is all that matters: while hardly enriching, it at least keeps some flicker of the soul alive. . . ." Her aim in life became defined; she determined not to let the poet that Osip had been, nor all they had lived through together, be lost. So Nadia carried Osip's poems, as well as his prose writings, and every scrap of their lives together, in her head. Night after night she recited his poems to herself, carrying this fragile treasure in the interior dark, month after month, year after year.

In 1956 she knew that age was weakening her, so she began to write the poems down in notebooks. Thus she rescued the writings of Osip Mandelstam, from both the Soviet police agents who sought to destroy them and from the Nazis. During World War II, the Nazis entered Voronezh and destroyed ninety-five percent of the town. But she had resourcefully given the notebooks to certain friends, who carried them away to safety on their persons.

During all these years, Osip Mandelstam remained in the history of Russian literature only as one who was "a non-person." This meant that his work could not be printed nor read, that it must be suppressed and destroyed whenever it turned up—all mention of him was to be deleted from literary sources.

Nadezhda, however, was as determined to preserve, as her society was determined to destroy, the poet's memory. "I could not have departed this life without telling something about the blithe soul who once lived at my side . . . about poetry. . . ."[19]

In her old age she was permitted to return to Moscow, and there she spent her last years writing everything down. One day she came across a letter she had written to Osip. "I wrote it in October 1938, and in January, I learned that M. was dead." The letter, thrown in a trunk, had remained there thirty years. ". . . what a joy it was living together like children—all our squabbles and arguments, the games we played, and our love. . . . Remember the way we brought back provisions to make our poor feasts in all the places where we pitched our tent like nomads? . . . Remember our happy poverty, and the poetry you wrote . . . . You are with me always, and I who was such a wild and angry one and never learned to weep simple tears—now I weep and weep and weep. It's me: Nadia. Where are you?"[20]

For a short time during the thaw under Khruschev the great poets and writers were to be "rehabilitated"—among them Osip Mandelstam. His name was restored to the records of the great Russian poets. But then the thaw hardened. The new Soviet edition of his books was stopped and remains unpublished.

But Nadezhda never gave up. She not only recorded from memory all his poems for future generations, but she wrote two extraordinary volumes of memoirs, the story of Osip and Nadezhda Mandelstam and their times. These works, unpublished in Russian, appeared simultaneously in Canada and the United States, published by Atheneum in New York in 1974, and translated from the Russian by Max Hayward, who also translated Pasternak and Solzhenitsyn.

In his Translator's Foreword Hayward writes of Nadezhda's commitment:

> In the years after his death, during all her painful wanderings from one dreary provincial town to another, her only aim in life was to be a living repository of his memory and his poetry, to preserve them from the total extinction to which they had been condemned. The publication of his work abroad (once attempts to have it published in the Soviet Union after Stalin's death had failed) and of the tale of what happened to him in *Hope Against Hope* are the fulfillment of Mrs. Mandelstam's pledge to keep her husband's name alive and to perpetuate what he left behind.[21]

Nadezhda Mandelstam was to hold fast to the belief in personal immortality: "If it were not for my faith in a future meeting I should never have been able to live through. . . . We shall meet, and there is no parting. Thus it was promised, and this is my faith."[22]

On December 19, 1980—forty-two years after Osip's death (almost to the day)—Nadezhda Mandelstam, aged eighty-one died in Moscow. The day after her death, the police "invaded her one-room apartment" and carried off her body. They declared that the State would bury her body since she had no surviving relatives. Her friends and legal heirs, who were making funeral arrangements at that very moment, were evicted from her rooms. The apartment was locked. But evidently they did not reckon with the iron determination of this woman. Her story does not end with this police action, and her tenacious will to rescue the life of imagination from oblivion triumphed even in her death.

Born into a Jewish family, Nadezhda Mandelstam had from her youth been an active communicant of the Russian Orthodox

Church. Her friends, who had been planning a religious burial according to her wishes, decided to follow Nadezhda's example and dig in their heels. They eventually managed to reclaim her body and the funeral took place in Moscow's Church of the Sign of the Holy Mother of God—"which was not large enough to accommodate all those who tried to get in."

A majority of those who tried to get in were the young. A new generation had been reading all the underground publications, including the poems of Osip Mandelstam and the writings of Nadezhda. They were hearing the voices of the poets and learning the things that Nadezhda strove to record, just for them—the new generations. That was the strange task which could have been brought to fulfillment only through this marriage.

9

Chanterelle and Shantidas

On a fine June day—it was the Feast of St. John the Baptist, June 24, 1948—the marriage of Joseph John Lanza del Vasto and Simone Gebelin was solemnized in the Gothic chapel of Crécy-en-Brie. Afterwards there was singing, chanting of psalms, and dancing in the beautiful garden of the cultured family who had made their estate available.

Fifty people came, though many times that number might have come, for the bridegroom was a famous spiritual teacher, and his books had a multitude of readers. The bride, too, had many friends in the world of music. She was a singer, her voice described as the purest of lyrical sopranos. They were a handsome couple—the man tall, ascetical looking, with deep blue eyes, and the tall, slender girl, dark-eyed, vividly vital. She wore a wedding gown she herself wove of fine white wool; he, too, wore a handwoven white wedding cloak with silver clasp.

Lanza del Vasto, called *Shantidas* by Mahatma Gandhi (meaning Servant of Peace), had also renamed Simone Gebelin when they met. He named her *Chanterelle* (meaning "bird call" or "the highest string of the violin"). Their friendship began with music. Then, after some time—one Palm Sunday following Mass and the joyful blessing of the branches—they told a large gathering of friends that they were betrothed. A shocked silence greeted them, no good wishes. Later Lanza realized that their companions had regarded him as a priest, and so his marriage announcement upset them. But there were still enough friends who rejoiced in the union of Shantidas and Chanterelle to fill the garden and make the air resound with music. They proclaimed their blessings and prayed for long life and many children. Indeed Shantidas and Chanterelle would have many children—at least one hundred and fifty. They were destined to create a unique family—the singing woman and the silent, disciple of Mahatma Gandhi.

In 1941 the German army, entering Paris, forced those who were anti-Nazi, among them most of the writers, artists, musicians, poets (and those Jews who had not already been swept up into internment camps) to seek refuge in Marseille. There, in the great port city, lived the family of Simone Gebelin, all musicians. They sold the famous pianos signed with their name. Her mother was Jewish, so Simone knew at an early age the significance of being different.

Their friends would come, together with the whole family, to sing—often singing in three, four, or six different parts at a first reading. One day a large young man appeared at the door. He said his name was Luc Dietrich, and he hoped they could share music. Simone welcomed him. He sang all the songs he knew; she knew them too, except one: "La Belle à la Fontaine." She asked, "Where did you find it?" Luc told her the song had been composed by "a certain Lanza." A few days later she went to visit Luc and found him sick in bed. Lanza was there, illuminating a manuscript. She had never met anyone like the tall, bearded man, thin from many fasts—and so silent. He spoke only about music, but she saw he knew nothing of music—yet he composed songs; they came to him when he walked. He brought her his music and she laughed, for the pages were covered with big, square, ridiculous, red notes. But when he sang the compositions they were beautiful, and she was determined to teach him "the grammar of music."

They met every Sunday, and on weekdays too, walking along the roads, singing and talking about music. She taught him to read music and set musical phrases to musical measures. Together they studied Gregorian chant, and on Sundays they sang together at

Mass, in the choir. Afterwards they would walk for hours and sing. Sometimes, carried away by song, they would kiss each other.

One spring day, after months of singing and studying together, Lanza appeared wearing a flowing black tie. He announced, "My first son is born!" Chanterelle was startled. She had assumed he was unmarried. "She knew nothing of me, not that I wrote, nor that I went on pilgrimages, in India and in the Holy Land, nor whence I came nor whither I was going; our friendship was exclusively musical," explained Lanza del Vasto later.

Seeing the bewilderment in her eyes, he quickly explained that he was talking about his first book. He held out the newly published volume to her. For the first time she learned who this man was, and of his pilgrimage to India, his discipleship with Mahatma Gandhi, his journey to Egypt and the Holy Land. A few months later, in the fall, he went away. He was working on another book, *Return to the Source.* It was published in France in 1943 and immediately sold thirty thousand copies. In the years that followed, *Return to the Source* was translated into many languages, finding millions of readers all over the world. Shantidas, Servant of Peace, became a name known wherever seekers for peace and justice survived.

The child baptized Joseph John Lanza del Vasto, born in 1901 in a village in southern Italy, came from a prominent family. His father, a Sicilian nobleman, had kings and even a sister of St. Thomas Aquinas among his ancestors. From boyhood Lanza del Vasto had questioned life. He studied philosophy and took his doctorate at the University of Pisa, writing his thesis on the Spiritual Trinity. His dissertation sought to reconcile aspects of Christian dogma, art, science, Carmelite contemplation, Hindu Yoga, Zen, and free speculation. Always he asked, "What is Life?" "Philosophy and all the sciences put together cannot account for the existence of a fly."

When the family fortunes collapsed, Lanza worked as an artist, making beautiful woodcarvings and other objects from ivory and metal. He led a seemingly carefree existence. But at thirty-five he went to India to seek Mahatma Gandhi, whom he considered a saint who "had rediscovered a truth that was capable of putting the soul back into life and renewing the world." *Satyagraha*—nonviolent love, "the force of justice . . . not a force applied to the defense of justice . . . a force inherent in justice itself."[1]

Lanza put on Indian garb and walked the roads as the local holy men did, wearing only a loincloth, carrying a begging bowl, fasting and singing. When he arrived at Gandhi's ashram in Wardha, Gandhi embraced him. Lanza said he had come to learn "how to be a better Christian." Gandhi's teaching had *work* at its center. Everyone must learn a craft, must work in the community, clean latrines, care for roads and streets, see that the water was not polluted, care for the sick, protect children and animals. Lanza liked the simple meals of the community, rice and vegetables, or two pancakes and a bowl of sour milk and brown sugar. He had gone to Gandhi in quest of Truth and was learning that Truth is not an abstraction. It is a life; it is a work; it is learning a skill; it is discipline and responsibility.

The Gandhian ideals of work and prayer were meant to change external power structures also, and the established government knew this. Gandhi and all who followed him were under constant police surveillance. Gandhi's teaching in response to surveillance was honesty: "Give the police all the information wanted, keep the police informed of your comings and goings, show the police your letters, and tell the police your secret thoughts. . . . It is a good way for us of making sure that we have only good thoughts."[2]

Gandhi, inspired by the Beatitudes of Christ, and by Tolstoy's writings on poverty and Christian love ("kindness and truth shall meet; justice and peace shall kiss"), wished to give to Christians a share in Hindu spirituality—it was a building up of God, not an exchange.

Lanza del Vasto wove his robe to wear on the pilgrimage that every pious Hindu undertakes once in life: to return to the source of the Ganges. When it was finished, Gandhi gave him his new name—Shantidas, Servant of Peace. So Lanza del Vasto set forth as Shantidas on a pilgrimage that was an ordeal. By the time he climbed to the source of the sacred river, his legs were swollen to half again their size by the bites of the poisonous flies, fever consumed him, his clothes were in rags. Deprived of strength, he lay down on the earth and felt he would never get up. As he lay there, memories of his childhood came—the beautiful white house with its terraces, his mother "standing on the tiled floor of the big room, her laughter echoing clear." He remembered his brothers, "there were three of us"—their beds side by side in the nursery. Lying in bed at night they would talk about life. "Why do we live? What happens when we sleep? And when we die?" The melancholy thought came to him: "What good has come to my mother from all the good she wished me? How have I rewarded the hopes of the mother who reared me with such delicate care?"[3]

In the morning a child came and left a bowl of rice for Lanza. The next day the child returned with a copper mug of tea and milk, and others came, treating him like a holy pilgrim, caring for him and reverencing him. Then the police came and arrested him for trespassing in forbidden territory. Weak and sick, he started back. On the way a priest gave him shelter in the Temple of Kali and asked him to talk of Christ. "He asked many questions and wanted to know all about Christ. So I talked to him of my Lord and my God." The priest, in turn, spoke of yoga. "Yoga moulds the body in a series of poses forming closed circuits." The secret lay in the practice of breathing and meditation: "Our body is the summing up of the whole creation, the only object we can know from inside at the same time as from outside."[4]

The sufferings he endured on this penitential pilgrimage—battered by the monsoons, starving, eaten by insects, sick, fasting—made him vulnerable to assaults of the demonic, and he understood why the saint "shouted more loudly than sinners, 'great is my sin'—not out of humility but out of the terror of the danger he knows only too well." Sanctity is the special target of the diabolic. Shantidas experienced temptations which St. Anthony, the desert father, wrote about, the temptations of obsessive sexuality, sensuality and despair. He had to recall why he was engaging in these extreme acts that could permanently destroy his body, "bring death, mutilation or permanent aberration."

He had come to India, not seeking adventure, but seeking truth and a way out of the disorder of modern life, the violence, the irreligion. He intended to finish his apprenticeship with Gandhi and then shut himself up in some Indian village and serve a general human cause. If he had done this, he might have been another "Mother Teresa"—going along the roads to rescue outcasts and abandoned people, the aged, the hopelessly ill, the unwanted dying infants. But his vocation was different. Gandhi sent him back to his own civilization to bring to the West the spirit of nonviolent action for peace and justice, *satyagraha*, to sow the good seed on "the most thankless of all ground—at home." He returned, going a long way around, via Egypt and Jerusalem.

"I returned from my pilgrimage unburdened of my errors and of my dreams, totally disarmed. . . . And twenty days after my return War broke out." World War II. Now he could practice nonviolence. Should it be some dramatic gesture? This was not what Gandhi taught; he said it was better to do something small. "The commonplace deed is a great step and a beautiful compromise. The beauty of it consists in today's compromise being less impure than yesterday's; it consists in our eyes being carried in a straight line towards something beautiful when we look, not at the deeds, but at the direction in which they are set." Gandhi taught that nothing is absolute in this world except the direction in which we advance "with a good will, sometimes uneasily and gropingly."[5]

To be a perfectionist about nonviolence, one would have to renounce eating, walking, breathing, living. "For eating is killing, walking is killing, breathing is killing. . . . Just as we cannot look the sun in the face, or see God face to face without dying, in the same way we cannot act out a single absolute in this world of appearances. . . . It is my very love for truth which has taught me the beauty of compromise,"[6] wrote Lanza del Vasto.

While he was in Switzerland he worked on a book about Gilles de Rais, a person who fascinated him. Gilles de Rais had accompanied Joan of Arc to Orleans. He had fought by her side, yet was not thereby saved from yielding to demonic temptations. He became rich and powerful, and would put on mystery and morality plays at his court; yet at the same time he was committing evil abominations. His servants kidnapped boys for him, whom he tortured and murdered. At last Gilles de Rais was brought to trial. His victims were said to number over one hundred and forty. He was hanged October 26, 1440. His story remained linked to that of the great saint, for both of these trials, Joan's and Gilles de Rais's came down together in the history of religion—the saint and the legendary Bluebeard—as the two most famous trials of the fifteenth century.

In researching Gilles de Rais, Lanza del Vasto discovered that the man had also been a musician who maintained choral groups and staged great chorales. Lanza discovered ballads which seemed all too familiar. He realized that these were the very songs and chants that came to him as he walked the mountains. He asked his friends to decipher the music in the old scripts. Amazed, his friends realized that the songs Lanza composed were like the songs of the ancient troubadours. Luc Dietrich suggested he compose a song for two voices, in the style of the old ballads—thus Lanza came to compose "La Belle à la Fontaine," which captivated Chanterelle.

Lanza del Vasto completed his book and returned to Paris. The book, *Return to the Source,* brought young people to him. In an old house in the St. Paul quarter of Paris, he spoke to them about the Gospels—in an original way. Chanterelle had also returned to Paris, and was studying Gregorian chant and counterpoint. She took her place with the group around Shantidas, and soon singing became an essential part of these meetings. Singing, said Lanza, is also gospel commentary. He suggested they call themselves "The Ark"—*L'Arche*—because they were like the animals in the Ark, coming together to live in peace.

But among traditionalists, some pious Catholics were shocked. An unauthorized lay person was commenting on the gospels! Not only that, but Shantidas was bringing ideas from India! He was relating gospel teachings to the struggle against injustice and underlining the gospel messages of justice and peace as spelled out by Christ. Pacifists were subversive. The pious accused him of distortions and wanted him silenced. Shantidas was concerned to be part of the continuity of the Church. He saw his Catholic and Roman heritage in a large, historical manner, as a slow growth across the centuries, with an innate affinity to and eventual incorporation of all good, wherever found. He said that the Ark was for all religions: "Our common prayer is addressed to the God of Truth, whom diverse men call by diverse names. . . ."[7]

The more "the establishment" found Shantidas suspect, the more the young were drawn to him. "What fascination does this man exercise over our young people?" The parents were sure he was a heretic, probably engaged in occult practices. Chanterelle was told by her priest to break off from the group. She begged her confessor to read her notes and see for himself what Shantidas was speaking. But he refused: "One does not discuss with the Devil," he said.

Chanterelle was too spirited to accept such an answer. She went to the Dominicans, whom she knew, and begged them to come and hear Lanza. For several months Dominican priests came and listened. Then they agreed: "There is nothing here contrary to the faith or morals." They even declared that Lanza del Vasto was saying what was in the gospels and necessary for our times. Later, when his commentaries on the gospels were published, Lanza del Vasto had no difficulty getting the imprimatur.

One day Shantidas returned from a walk to find a note: "Gandhi was killed today. I am committed to you with all my life." It was from Chanterelle. The following Sunday, as they walked the country roads, Lanza declared "I am going to say something to you that I have never said to any person: I love you more than my solitude. I ask you to be my wife."

"No, no, my friend," cried Chanterelle. She began to weep, and explained that her health had always been frail and that she would only be a burden to him. Lanza lifted her up and jumped up, holding her, three high jumps, singing, "See how you burden me!" He told her that even though he could pick her up and leap in the air with her, it would actually be her strength that he needed to carry him, "your love which has no weakness in it."

Friends and patrons had offered Shantidas a place to begin the first experiment in community. Charles Fauconnier offered them a large piece of land with a kitchen garden and a wing of the house for their living quarters, plus the same salary that Fauconnier had given a German prisoner of war who had served as caretaker of the farm, but had since been repatriated. It was there, in the garden, that Shantidas and Chanterelle had their wedding celebration. And there, at Tournier, the first foundation, *L'Arche* (the Ark), was established. *L'Arche* also means "arch"—the arch of the rainbow, symbolizing God's promise of safe passage over stormy seas, the brilliant light suddenly appearing out of dark clouds. Shantidas also perceived that the arch was the Vine that would bring forth good fruit.

And their marriage did bring forth communities of peacemakers. Not in her wildest dreams had Chanterelle imagined such a mate, nor herself as mother to such a family. Blessed are the peacemakers. But "a peacemaker does not mean a peaceful person . . . peacemakers make peace . . . out of disorder," warned Lanza del Vasto. To the community of the Ark, established at Tournier in 1948, came peacemakers who had no notion of the scriptural meaning of peace or peacemaking.

As a small child Chanterelle, like Lanza had been a questioning person. Standing in front of the window, staring at the design in the lace curtains, she would ask, "Why this design? What does it mean? And I? Why am I here?" Staring out at people in the street, she asked the same question: "Where are they going?" She felt alone, the only one who did not know where she was going. Her questioning mind made her a good student, but she soon saw that neither her teachers nor the books could answer her questions. When she graduated from secondary school, she felt she knew nothing. Though Chanterelle's spirit was joyful by nature, and she was surrounded by loving parents, a sister, friends, and a home filled with music, she was troubled and kept asking herself what life was all about. In her experience religious teachings spoke only of sin and hellfire, rarely of love.

Although Chanterelle and her sister were baptized as infants to fulfill their mother's promise to their Catholic father, sometimes she would follow her grandmother to the synagogue. And at school, Chanterelle discovered deep-seated prejudices everywhere—the disgust of Catholics for Jews was responded to with disgust of Jews for Catholics. She was perturbed that all sincerely religious people, springing from the same great Judeo-Christian root, having memorized the Commandments and the Beatitudes, seemed to produce more of the bitter fruit of hate than the sweet fruit of love! The only place she felt God near was in the midst of nature, when she was walking in the country and singing songs.

But this did not altogether satisfy her. Singing of the glory of God in the forest and hearing the wind sing the glory of God in the trees were inspiring, but did not answer the great questions about life. At night, when she returned home and closed the door behind her, she would go to the window, look out at the street full of people, noise, city lights, and ask, "Who am I?" "Why am I here?"

On the surface she was full of joy and liveliness, but underneath there was deep unrest, even anguish. When she was twenty Chanterelle had a mystical experience of Christ. In the wake of this experience, she decided to be a nurse. In the hospital, with people who were suffering and complaining, praying and groaning, she felt closer to God. But her health was not up to the hard work, and she fell ill and had to leave.

With a friend she went to Italy. There, in the churches, she felt inspired. She saw Christ as the greatest artists pictured him, imagery vast and stirring. She kept going back to the churches, looking at Christ with arms open to include her, or at the Risen Christ blessing her. She pondered these experiences. Why did she, who felt herself a stranger in the world, feel at home here? His house seemed to be her house. She began going to daily Mass, but the contradictions within the Church, between teaching and practice, troubled her.

"Where in all this are my brother Jews?" she asked. "And all the others . . . the outsiders? What is their place in the all-embracing Christ love?" When she returned to France she went to see her friends, the Dominicans. One became her spiritual director. He told her, "Pray and you will understand."

So it was that Simone Gebelin, during the same years that Lanza del Vasto was in quest of Truth, was traveling the same interior trail. Then came World War II and the Occupation of France, the raids by the German storm troopers seeking Jews and dissidents, and the flight of the artists to Marseille—and the meeting of Shantidas and Chanterelle. All the gropings of her life seemed to lead to this encounter. In the months they studied music together, especially Gregorian chant, she experienced the contemplative joy of understanding through prayer that her Dominican spiritual director had talked about. Her childhood ponderings and questions bore the telltale mark of the true contemplative, but without direction she had been at the mercy of all the winds, wandering up and down the earth—not outwardly as Lanza had done, but inwardly—seeking.

Now, as Chanterelle sang the chants of praise, the psalms and the liturgy, she entered into the Sacrifice of Christ in the Mass and "was lifted up almost palpably," understanding the joy of St. John of the Cross and St. Francis of Assisi. "Yes, it is all a deep mystery. . . . We do not know whence we come or whither we go. God alone shows us the way, the birth and the sacrifice, the gift of self unto death, and the resurrection in glory, all these enclose our life—like the circle of the Gregorian chant, the musical theme which repeats and counterpoints and returns with the same theme," she wrote.

Chanterelle and Shantidas were two contemplatives, taking each other by the hand and stepping onto the swaying bridge, delicate as a tightrope or a spider's thread, that spans the chasm between the human and divine. It was not idle romanticism. It was a Work! "If you wish to understand the Gospels," said Shantidas, "it is necessary for you to live the Gospels, not just to hear the Gospels; it is necessary for you to search out the truth that can only be found by you yourself through interior clarity."[8]

The body is our given instrument, Shantidas taught, and must be prepared for this work of understanding and living. The nerves must be relaxed, the intellect quieted, the heart purified. Breathing was a vital discipline in preparation. We live on air, said Shantidas, even more than on bread. "We are born with our first breath and die with our last."

Years later, writing in the periodical of the community of the Ark, *Nouvelles De L'Arche* (*News of the Ark*), Chanterelle noted, "The principal thing is to be committed to the Way. There are many boulders (imaginary, says Shantidas), but they must be surmounted to reach interior unity and charity. Gropingly we advance holding each other by the hand."

There were boulders which sometimes seemed more like mountains. They could not be climbed over; they had to be gone around, patiently. The first community at Tournier drew a great many people; all had their own ideas about peace and love and freedom. They were all masters without ever having been disciples first.

"There were some fine people in the group, but Tournier became hell," said Shantidas. "There was a huge flow of newcomers all the time. We took in anybody. *Anybody.* Most of them were the wrong people." A free community without a rule of life could soon become chaos. "In ordinary life you have laws and institutions, you call in the police to settle disputes. We had no such recourse."

After five years they abandoned Tournier and made a fresh start, with a strict rule of life, near Bollène. One who wished to enter the community was a novice for three years, and then could only be admitted permanently by unanimous vote. It was an "order"—but not a religious order. "It is at the same time a working order," wrote Shantidas, "and a school of the inner life. . . ."

As the community grew, more space was needed. After ten years they acquired two thousand acres of land in the Cavenne Mountains of Languedoc, space enough for several communities. Branches of the Ark sprang up in Morocco, Belgium, Canada, and Argentina, and throughout Europe and the United States there were "Friends of the Ark." They organized seminars to teach the life of nonviolence, with the same application to all levels of existence.

Chanterelle compared the spiritual techniques to those of the musician, only the instrument was the human body. Like the violin, it must be tuned. Shantidas expressed the essential theme that their way was "a Life," not merely a preparation for something else. It was intrinsically a good way to live.

The family gathered after common prayer each night around the fire to renew their vows of prayer, silence, meditation, work and service, responsibility, poverty, purification, truthfulness and non-violence. They also vowed to make dignity and beauty where there was contempt and ugliness, and their lives bore fruit. The time of ripeness came and they went out into the world to the places where the fever of human injustice to fellow beings burned hottest. Like the people in the Bible, they went into the heart of the fiery furnace, off to Paris, where they chained themselves to railings around the obelisk in the Place de la Concorde, to protest the atrocities in the war between France and Algeria.

"Three very thin men, bearded and dressed in brown trousers and blue smocks," wrote the reporter on the Paris *L'Express,* "canvas shoes on their bare feet . . . began a public twenty-day fast on the thirty-first of March. Until the Eve of Easter Sunday, they will take nothing but water. . . . The reason for their voluntary ordeal is the Algerian war and the atrocities perpetrated on both sides."[9]

The community undertook many such fasts, protests, and demonstrations. They fasted against nuclear war, the atomic bomb, internment camps, torture, and imprisonment and injustice.

On March 4, 1963, Shantidas went to Rome for The Great Rome Fast. There he wrote a long letter to the new Pope, John XXIII, who had inspired renewed hope in peacemakers. In his letter Shantidas asked the Pope for "the message of peace the whole world needs today, the bold, absolute, in short, the evangelical word. . . . Who will protect God's creation and all the beauty and goodness it contains against covetousness, fear and pride . . . who, if not the Church, *mater et magistra*?"[10]

The letter pleaded for a concrete statement embodying the principle of spiritual resistance. After sending it off, Shantidas went into seclusion in the Cistercian convent at Frattocchio, the monastery at the foot of the Alban Hills to begin his forty-day fast.

No answer came, only an official acknowledgment came from the Vatican twenty days later. On Palm Sunday, Chanterelle arrived. On Holy Wednesday she visited the Secretary of State, taking with her yet another letter, requesting an answer to the first and a blessing for Holy Week. The Secretary talked with her for over an hour and told her that the letter had indeed been read. "The answer is here!" he said, and handed her the encyclical *Pacem In Terris,* which would be published the next day.

"There are things in it," he assured her, "that have never been said, pages that might have been signed by your husband!"[11]

On Good Friday, as Shantidas was on the terrace, a priest arrived. "I've brought you some news from the Vatican." He presented Lanza with gifts from the Pope—two leather cases bearing the papal arms and containing a rosary and a medal, with an accompanying message, the special prayer of Pope John XXIII for Shantidas and Chanterelle.

In 1965 it was Chanterelle who went to Rome to fast for ten days. She went with a group of twenty Catholic and Protestant women from different countries, women who declared they were in Rome "in support of the Council." They went into seclusion in the Convent of the Last Supper to fast and pray for messages seeking a halt to the arms race and atom bombs. "Dorothy Day, to our great joy, came and fasted in Rome with us," Chanterelle wrote.

She kept a diary and therein recorded the days of their fasting:

> Once through the gate we found a small group of joyful women waiting in the courtyard. They were the fasters. . . . We let Dorothy Day, who is elderly, and Erika Mitterer, the writer, each have a single, sunny room, and the others settled in two by two according to friendships struck up on the spur of the moment. . . . Our fast is not public. It is neither protest nor pressure, but on the contrary, an act of piety, penance, and union. . . .[12]

The first hungry days were not easy. Chanterelle wrote, "Suffer suffering to come unto me. The big beast spreads itself slowly astonished. . . . We let it come in. It lies down full length and stretches out its long legs. Sickness grips you. Thanks be to God, this is what we wanted. In vain does it weigh on the heart and the pit of the stomach, no one makes a gesture to push it off. Thanks to it, we feel what thousands of human beings feel, weak and starving. Thanks be to God."[13]

As each day passed, Chanterelle wrote in her diary that each fasting person "after a period of melancholy, finds her good humor again and straightens herself again like a flower. A lesson on nonviolence. Suffer suffering to come unto me, say Yes, understand, suffer, and most conflict disappears. It is the first stage in the great adventure." The Very Reverend Father Abbot visited the fasting women to thank them. He said, "The Council is not a meeting of dignitaries laying down the law, it is you! It is God's people suffering, hoping, and praying."[14]

When the Statement by the Council was issued, the women saw that their prayers and fasts had borne astonishing fruit. People all around the world had been fasting with them, not just in the communities that were branches of the Ark, but in parishes where the fast had been announced and commented on. And in Schema XIII, Chapter V, the statement they had been praying for appeared; they read their very sentences, declaring forthright embrace of the spirit of nonviolence.

Chanterelle and Shantidas had built an Ark over which an ancient rainbow arched. Their family was biblical, and it had increased and multiplied. Chanterelle saw the whole human family in microcosm—it was also the Tree of Life. She thought of the journey she and Shantidas had made to his birthplace in Italy. As she watched him addressing a large gathering in the room of the great house where he had been born, she saw simultaneously the small fair-haired child and the white-haired man, to whom all were listening so intently. He was speaking of Bernardone, the father of Saint Francis of Assisi. The parable of Francis was a parable of themselves. They, too, had to break with their old family and go forth and start a new family.

She recalled how she had also had to leave her past, her mother and father, and her old ways of thinking, when she cast her lot with

Shantidas. She had been called to take up her pallet and walk, as the parable of the paralytic admonished. And she realized how her search for meaning, her longing to live this life in a way worth living had been answered when she accepted the offer of marriage from this man.

Shantidas expressed their unity in an essay he wrote about marriage: "The earth has two poles and man has two poles which are man and woman . . . and woman has two poles, of which one is man-in-her, and man has two, of which one is the woman-in-him. . . . Everything that walks moves by the alternation of right and left . . . supreme happiness, goodness and rightness, life itself is that unity."[15] "Marriage is not a state in life; it is a Work." It is the effort to unify all the elements within the self and to be united with the other.

As the years passed, Chanterelle's health became more fragile. Nevertheless, she gave herself with the same wholeness to those in need, and she sang with the same ardent energy her ascending high notes, and she hospitably welcomed visitors and saw to their comforts. Visitors described the room where Shantidas and Chanterelle lived. It was a studio, study and living room and bedroom, filled with books and works of art, many of which they had made. "The large double bed was covered with a spread woven in many colors, and the bed legs were beautifully carved. Over the fireplace hung the guitar he had taken to India on his first pilgrimage."[16]

In the fall of 1975, as the leaves changed color, withered, and dropped from the trees, the birdlike singer lay dying. Chanterelle died on November 12. "Shantidas lost his beloved life-partner. . . . The death of the woman whose buoyant spirit and joyous voice has sustained the Ark from its very beginning shocked the community profoundly."[17]

Chanterelle's last letter to the Companions, the family in the Ark, recalled how she and Shantidas had embarked together and how difficulties had never been lacking. But they had had each other, and had groped their way, hand in hand. Now she was approaching God, alone. "Je suis enfin seule devant Toi seul." (I am at last alone before Thee alone.)

Shantidas's epitaph for Chanterelle needs to be read in its original French:

Epitaphe

Ici finit
Ce qui porta le nom de Chanterelle
Son visage et sa voix. Passant priez pour elle.
Ici l'oiseau chanteur à fait son dernier nid
Et puis s'est envolé haut, plus haut que son aile.
Alleluia

Shantidas.

The words *Ici finit* cannot be translated into English as "here ends," for only this part of Chanterelle's story was ended.

In English the epitaph might be translated:

Epitaph

Here leaves off
She who bore the name of Chanterelle
Her looks and her voice. Passerby pray for her.
Here the singing bird has made her last nest
And then flew up high, higher still, beyond her own wings.
Alleluia

Shantidas.

Emily Dickinson used a strangely similar metaphor of the bird flying up out of the nest at the end of life on this plane. She wrote, "What indeed is Earth but a Nest, from whose rim we are all falling?"

The bird falls from the nest and must catch the current and fly skyward. It must not be a weak-winged fledgling, but with strong wings, growing stronger in the practice of the flight, it must soar up alone, beyond her own capacity. For this moment of flight all alone, Chanterelle and Shantidas had been practicing together.

Shantidas died in Spain on January 5, 1981. He was visiting a new foundation of the community and had not been feeling well. He was in bed, reading poetry, when the fatal cerebral hemorrhage struck. He died a few hours later. The Spanish Basque woman, Mayte, who had been with Chanterelle at her death, was there. Shantidas had left instructions for what he wanted done when he died:

... mes enfants, quand j'aurais rendu l'âme,
couchez-moi de côte dans la tombe,
Liez bien la sandale à mon pied,
mettez bien le bâton dans mon poins,
car je veux être prêt au lever,
Quand viendra Celui qui doit venir.[18]

He asked to be placed in the tomb with his sandals on his feet and his baton in his hands: "I wish to be ready to rise up when The One comes who must come."

Notes

Chapter 1 / Catherine and William Blake

1. Thomas Craven, *Men of Art* (New York: Simon and Schuster, 1931), p. 359.
2. W. B. Yeats, ed., *Poems of William Blake* (New York: The Modern Library, 1930), p. 181.
3. *Ibid.,* p. 137.
4. *Ibid.,* p. xxiii.
5. *Ibid.,* p. 137.
6. *Ibid.,* p. 77.
7. *Ibid.,* p. 93.
8. *Ibid.,* p. 103.
9. *Ibid.,* p. 136.
10. *Ibid.,* p. xxxix.

> *Other sources consulted:*
>
> J. Bronowski, *William Blake and the Age of Revolution* (New York: Harper and Row).
> O. Burdett, *William Blake, English Men of Letters Series.* (New York: Macmillan, 1926).
> A. C. Swinburne, *William Blake: A Critical Study* (London: Heinemann, 1925).
> Mark Van Doren, *Anthology of World Poetry* (New York: Albert and Charles Boni, 1929).

Chapter 2 / Frances and Gilbert Chesterton

1. Maisie Ward, *Gilbert Keith Chesterton* (New York: Sheed & Ward, 1943), p. 396.
2. *Ibid.,* p. 416.

3. G. K. Chesterton, *St. Francis of Assisi* (New York: Doubleday & Co., 1924), p. 72.
4. Ward, *op. cit.,* p. 84.
5. *Ibid.,* p. 86.
6. *Ibid.,* p. 540.
7. *Ibid.,* p. 284.
8. *Ibid.,* p. 537.
9. *Ibid.,* p. 653.

Other sources consulted:
Richard Aldington, *The Viking Book of Poetry of the English Speaking World* (New York, 1941).
G. K. Chesterton, *The Everlasting Man* (New York: Image Books).
————, *Orthodoxy* (New York: Image Books).
————, *Saint Thomas Aquinas* (New York: Image Books).
Emile Legouis and L. Cazamian, *A History of English Literature* (London: J. M. Dent & Sons, 1927).

Chapter 3 / Maisie Ward and Frank Sheed

1. Maisie Ward, *Unfinished Business* (New York: Sheed & Ward, 1964), p. 121.
2. Frank Sheed, *The Church and I* (New York: Doubleday, 1974), p. 107.
3. Ward, *op. cit.,* p. 87.
4. *Ibid.,* p. 3.
5. Frank Sheed, *The Instructed Heart* (Huntington, Ind.: *Our Sunday Visitor,* 1979), p. 18.
6. Ward, *op. cit.,* p. 87.
7. *Ibid.,* p. 41.
8. Sheed, *op. cit.,* p. 11.
9. *Ibid.,* p. 13.
10. Ward, *op. cit.,* p. 81.
11. Sheed, *The Church and I,* p. 87.
12. *Ibid.,* p. 11; see also Ward, *op. cit.,* pp. 132–133.
13. *Ibid.,* p. 11.
14. *Ibid.,* p. 14.
15. *Ibid.,* p. 15.
16. *Ibid.,* p. 37.
17. *Ibid.,* p. 40.
18. *Ibid.,* p. 43.
19. *Ibid.,* pp. 42–43.
20. *Ibid.,* p. 43.

21. *Ibid.,* p. 84.
22. *Ibid.,* p. 86.
23. Ward, *op. cit.,* pp. 103–104.
24. Sheed, *The Church and I,* p. 107.
25. Ward, *op. cit.,* p. 113.
26. *Ibid.,* pp. 114–115.
27. *Ibid.,* p. 123.
28. *Ibid.,* p. 124.
29. *Ibid.,* p. 131.
30. *Ibid.,* p. 137.
31. Sheed, *The Church and I,* p. 110.
32. *Ibid.,* pp. 124, 247.
33. Ward, *op. cit.,* p. 146.
34. *Ibid.,* p. 153.
35. Sheed, *The Church and I,* p. 160.
36. *Ibid.,* p. 178.
37. Sheed, *The Instructed Heart,* pp. 7, 8.

Other sources consulted:

Maisie Ward, *Caryll Houselander, That Divine Eccentric* (New York: Sheed and Ward, 1962).

———, *To and Fro on the Earth* (New York: Sheed and Ward, 1973).

Chapter 4 / Olivia and Samuel Clemens

1. Dixon Wecter, ed., *The Love Letters of Mark Twain* (New York: Harper Brothers, 1949), p. 62.
2. *Ibid.,* p. 144.
3. *Ibid.,* p. 209.
4. *Ibid.,* p. 265.
5. *Ibid.,* p. 328.
6. Mark Twain adapted the verse by an Australian poet for the stone marking the grave of Olivia Susan Clemens.
7. Edward Wagenknecht, *Mark Twain: The Man and His Works* (New Haven: Yale University Press, 1935), p. 212.

Other sources consulted:

Van Wyck Brooks, *The Ordeal of Mark Twain* (New York: E. P. Dutton, 1920).

Clara Clemens, *My Father, Mark Twain* (New York: Harper Brothers, 1931).

Cyril Clemens, a personal letter to the authors, July, 1980.

————, "The True Character of Mark Twain's Wife," *Missouri Historical Review,* no. 24 (1929).

Stephen Leacock, *Mark Twain* (New York: Appleton & Co., 1933).

Albert Bigelow Paine, *A Short Life of Mark Twain* (New York: Harper Brothers, 1920).

Mark Twain, *Autobiography* (New York: Harper Brothers, 1924).

Chapter 5 / Nora and James Joyce

1. Richard Ellmann, *James Joyce, A Biography* (New York: Oxford University Press, 1959), p. 102.
2. *Ibid.,* p. 165.
3. *Ibid.,* p. 166.
4. Padraic and Mary Colum, *Our Friend James Joyce* (Magnolia, Mass.: Peter Smith Press, 1958), p. 206.
5. Ellmann, *op. cit.,* pp. 175, 177.
6. *Ibid.,* p. 180.
7. Colum, *op. cit.,* p. 206.
8. *Ibid.,* p. 185.
9. Ellmann, *op. cit.,* p. 212.
10. *Ibid.,* p. 384.
11. *Ibid.,* p. 237.
12. *Ibid.*
13. *Ibid.,* p. 289.
14. *Ibid.,* p. 291.
15. *Ibid.,* p. 349.
16. *Ibid.,* p. 540.
17. *Ibid.,* p. 588 (footnote).
18. *Ibid.,* p. 390.
19. *Ibid.,* p. 572.
20. *Ibid.,* pp. 688, 689.
21. Colum, *op. cit.,* pp. 114, 115.

Other sources consulted:

Zack Bowen, *Padraic Colum, A Biographic-Critical Introduction* (Carbondale and Edwardsville, Ill.: Southern Illinois Press, 1970).

Mary Colum, *Life and the Dream* (New York, 1947).

Richard Ellmann, *The Consciousness of Joyce* (New York: Oxford University Press, 1977).

Kevin Sullivan, *Joyce among the Jesuits* (New York: Columbia University Press, 1958).

Chapter 6 / Paula and Martin Buber

1. Martin Buber, *A Believing Humanism: My Testament* (New York: Credo Perspectives, Simon and Schuster, 1967), p. 49.
2. Aubrey Hodes, *Martin Buber: An Intimate Portrait* (New York: The Viking Press, 1971), p. 43.

Other sources consulted:

Martin Buber, *Between Man and Man* (New York: Macmillan, 1965).

———, *Hasidism* (New York: Philosophical Library, 1948).

———, *I and Thou* (New York: Charles Scribner's Sons, 1958).

———, *Tales of the Hasidim: Later Masters* (New York: Schocken Books, 1948).

Maurice Friedman, Buber scholar, personal interviews.

———, "The Intellectual Challenge Buber Left Us," *Thought,* vol. 53, no. 210 (September, 1978).

———, *The Hidden Human Image* (New York: Delta, 1975).

John M. Oesterreicher, *The Hasidic Movement,* (New York: Pantheon Books, 1958).

Chapter 7 / Raissa and Jacques Maritain

1. Raissa Maritain, *Raissa's Journal.* Presented by Jacques Maritain (Albany, N.Y.: Magi Books, 1974), p. 311.
2. *Ibid.,* p. 274.
3. Raissa Maritain, *We Have Been Friends Together* (New York: Longmans, Green and Co., 1942), p. 25.
4. *Ibid.,* p. 26.
5. *Ibid.,* p. 40.
6. *Ibid.,* p. 41.
7. *Ibid.,* p. 76.
8. *Ibid.,* pp. 77–78.
9. *Ibid.,* pp. 96–97.
10. *Ibid.,* p. 106.
11. *Ibid.,* p. 118.
12. *Ibid.,* p. 119.
13. *Ibid.,* p. 123 (see also footnote).
14. *Ibid.,* p. 143.
15. *Ibid.,* p. 144.
16. *Raissa's Journal,* p. 8.
17. *Ibid.,* p. 300.

18. Jacques Maritain, *Existence and the Existent* (New York: Doubleday, 1956), p. 80.
19. *We Have Been Friends Together*, p. 192.
20. *Raissa's Journal*, p. 400.
21. *Ibid.*, pp. 8, 13.
22. *Ibid.*, p. 92.
23. *Ibid.*, p. 276.
24. *Ibid.*, p. 277.
25. *Ibid.*, p. 255.
26. *We Have Been Friends Together*, p. 173.
27. *Raissa's Journal*, p. 401.
28. *Ibid.*, p. 292.
29. *Ibid.*, pp. 309–10.
30. Julie Kernan, *Our Friend Jacques Maritain* (New York: Doubleday, 1975), p. 47.
31. Erik H. Erikson, *Gandhi's Truth* (New York: W. W. Norton Co., 1969), p. 22.
32. *Raissa's Journal*, p. 9.
33. *Our Friend Jacques Maritain*, pp. 140–45.
34. *Raissa's Journal*, p. 9.
35. *Our Friend Jacques Maritain*, p. 174.
36. *Ibid.*, p. 178.

Chapter 8 / Nadezhda and Osip Mandelstam

1. Elena Malits, "Thomas Merton and the Possibilities of Religious Imagination," *The Message of Thomas Merton*, ed. Brother Patrick Hart (Kalamazoo, Mi.: Cistercian Publications, 1981), p. 50.
2. Nadezhda Mandelstam, *Hope Abandoned* (New York: Atheneum, 1974), p. 11.
3. *Ibid.*, p. 136.
4. *Ibid.*, p. 11.
5. *Ibid.*, p. 180.
6. *Ibid.*, p. 20.
7. *Ibid.*, p. 126.
8. Clarence Brown, *Mandelstam* (New York: Cambridge University Press, 1973), p. 37.
9. Mandelstam, *op. cit.*, p. 128.
10. *Ibid.*, p. 260.
11. *Ibid.*, p. 195.
12. *Ibid.*, p. 261.

13. *Ibid.,* p. 16.
14. *Ibid.,* pp. 489–91.
15. *Ibid.,* p. 629.
16. *Ibid.,* p. 294.
17. *Ibid.,* p. 608.
18. *Ibid.,* p. 144.
19. *Ibid.,* p. 608.
20. *Ibid.,* pp. 620–21.
21. *Ibid.,* p. vii.
22. *Ibid.,* p. 265.

Chapter 9 / Chanterelle and Shantidas

1. Lanza del Vasto, *Return to the Source* (New York: Schocken Books, 1972), p. 40.
2. *Ibid.,* p. 124.
3. *Ibid.,* p. 198.
4. *Ibid.,* pp. 213–17.
5. Lanza del Vasto, *Gandhi to Vinoba* (New York: Schocken Books, 1974), p. 64.
6. *Ibid.,* p. 64.
7. *Ibid.,* p. 137.
8. Lanza del Vasto, *Make Straight the Way of the Lord* (New York: Alfred A. Knopf, 1974), pp. 3, 4, 97, 253.
9. ————, *Warriors of Peace* (New York: Alfred A. Knopf, 1974), pp. x, xi, xii, 61, 77.
10. *Ibid.,* pp. 165, 168.
11. *Ibid.,* pp. 170–71.
12. *Ibid.,* pp. 178, 181.
13. *Ibid.,* pp. 184–85.
14. *Ibid.,* p. 189.
15. *Make Straight the Way of the Lord,* p. 41.
16. Marjorie Hope and James Young, *The Struggle for Humanity* (New York: Orbis Books), pp. 49–61.
17. *Ibid.,* pp. 49, 61.
18. Jane Prentiss, from a personal letter to the authors, quoting Yvette Naal, on the death of Shantidas and his expressed wishes—which Jane Prentiss quoted in French, and we translated after giving the exact statement in French.

All biographical material in this narrative comes from personal interviews by letter, and further correspondence with Yvette Naal, Shantidas' secretary, and from copies of the periodical published by the Community of The Ark (La Borie Noble, 34260 le Bousquet d'Orb, France—*Nouvelles de l'Arche,* particularly the issue of *Année XVI Eté* 1968, Numéro 10, *la porte ouverte,* "Chanterelle" by herself).

Bibliography

Aldington, R., ed. *Viking Book of Poetry*. New York: Viking, 1941.

Blake, William. *Poems of William Blake*. Edited by W. B. Yeats. New York: Modern Library, 1930.

————. *Poetical Works*. Edited by J. Sampson. London: Oxford University Press, 1905.

————. *Songs of Innocence and Experience*. Chicago: Doubleday, 1916.

Bloy, Léon. *Pilgrim of the Absolute*. Introduction by Jacques Maritain. New York: Pantheon Books, 1947.

Bowen, Zack. *Padraic Colum, A Biographic-Critical Introduction*. Carbondale and Edwardsville, Ill.: Southern Illinois Press, 1970.

Bronoski, J. *William Blake and the Age of Revolution*. New York: Harper & Row, 1969.

Brooks, Van Wyck. *The Ordeal of Mark Twain*. New York: Dutton, 1920.

Brown, Clarence. *Mandelstam*. New York: Cambridge University Press, 1973.

Buber, Martin. *A Believing Humanism*. New York: Simon & Schuster, 1967.

————. *Between Man and Man*. New York: Macmillan, 1965.

————. *Eclipse of God*. New York: Harper & Row, 1957.

————. *Hasidism*. New York: Philosophical Library, 1948.

————. *I and Thou*. New York: Philosophical Library, 1948.

————. *The Knowledge of Man*. New York: Harper & Row, 1966.

————. *Letters of Martin Buber*. New York: Schocken, 1963.

————. *My Road to Hasidism*. New York: Schocken, 1965.

————. *Tales of the Hasidim*. New York: Macmillan, 1965.

Bunyan, John. *Pilgrim's Progress*. Illustrations by William Blake. New York: Heritage, 1942.

Burdett, D. *William Blake*. New York: Macmillan, 1926.

Carlisle, Olga. *Solzhenitsyn and the Secret Circle*. Holt, Rinehart & Winston, 1976.

Chesterton, G. K. *Autobiography*. New York: Sheed & Ward, 1936.

———. *Blake*. New York: Dutton, 1910.

———. *The Everlasting Man*. New York: Image Books, 1955.

———. *Orthodoxy*. New York: Image Books, 1954.

———. *St. Francis of Assisi*. New York: Doubleday, 1924.

———. *St. Thomas Aquinas*. New York: Image Books, 1956.

Clemens, Clara. *My Father, Mark Twain*. New York: Harper & Row, 1931.

Clemens, Cyril. *Mark Twain Journal*. Missouri, 1980.

———. Personal letter to the authors, 1981.

———. "The True Character of Mark Twain's Wife," *Missouri Review*, 1929.

Cohen, Arthur A. *Martin Buber*. New York: Hillary House, 1957.

Colum, Mary. *Life and the Dream*. New York: 1947.

Colum, Padraic and Mary. *Our Friend James Joyce*. Magnolia, Mass.: Peter Smith Press, 1958.

Craven, Thomas. *Men of Art*. New York: Simon & Schuster, 1931.

De Lancey, Ferguson, *Mark Twain: Man and Legend*. New York: Bobbs-Merrill Company, 1943.

Del Vasto, Lanza. *Gandhi to Vinoba*. New York: Schocken Books, 1974.

———. *Make Straight the Way of the Lord*. New York: Knopf, 1974.

———. *Return to the Source*. New York: Schocken Books, 1972.

———. *Warriors of Peace*. New York: Knopf, 1974.

De Voto, Bernard. *Mark Twain's America*. New York: Little, Brown and Company, 1933.

Ellis, E. J. *The Real Blake*. New York: Doubleday, 1907.

Ellmann, Richard. *The Consciousness of Joyce*. New York: Oxford University Press, 1977.

———. *James Joyce, A Biography*. New York: Oxford University Press, 1959.

Erikson, Erik. *Gandhi's Truth*. New York: W. W. Norton Co., 1969.

Evans, Joseph W., ed. *Jacques Maritain: The Man and His Achievement*. New York: Sheed & Ward, 1963.

Friedman, Maurice. *The Hidden Image*. New York: Delta, 1975.

———. "The Intellectual Challenge of Buber," *Thought*, vol. 53, 1978.

Green, Roger Lancelyn and Hooper, Walter. *C. S. Lewis: A Biography*. New York: Harcourt Brace Jovanovich, 1974.

Griffin, John Howard and Simon, Yves R. *Jacques Maritain, Homage in Words and Pictures*. Albany, New York: Magi Books, 1974.

Hodes, Aubrey, *Mark Twain, An Intimate Portrait*. New York: Viking, 1971.

Hope, Marjorie and Young, James. *The Struggle for Humanity*. New York: Orbis Books, 1977.

Kernan, Julie. *Our Friend Jacques Maritain*. New York: Doubleday & Co., 1975.

Leacock, Stephen. *Mark Twain*. New York: Appleton, 1933.

Le Conte, Edward. *Grace to a Witty Sinner*. New York: Walker 1965.

Legouis and Cazamian. *A History of English Literature.* London: Dent, 1927.

Lewis, C. S. *A Grief Observed.* New York: The Seabury Press, 1961.

————. *Surprised by Joy.* New York: Harcourt, Brace & World, 1955.

Lewis, W. H., ed. *Letters of C. S. Lewis,* with a Memoir by W. H. Lewis. New York: Harcourt, Brace & World, 1966.

Malits, Elena. "Thomas Merton and the Possibilities of Religious Imagination" in *The Message of Thomas Merton,* edited by Brother Patrick Hart. Kalamazoo, Michigan: Cistercian Publications, 1981.

Mandelstam, Nadezhda. *Hope Abandoned.* New York: Atheneum, 1974.

————. *Hope Against Hope.* New York: Atheneum, 1970.

Mariani, Paul. *William Carlos Williams: A New World Naked.* New York: McGraw-Hill, 1981.

Maritain, Jacques. *Art and Poetry.* New York: Philosophical Library, 1943.

————. *Art and Scholasticism.* New York: Charles Scribner's, 1960.

————. *Existence and the Existent.* New York: Doubleday, 1956.

Maritain, Raissa. *Adventures in Grace.* New York, 1940.

————. *Raissa's Journal.* Presented by Jacques Maritain. Albany, New York: Magi Books, Inc., 1974.

————. *We Have Been Friends Together.* New York: Longmans, Green & Co., 1942.

Milton, John. *Paradise Lost.* Illustrations by William Blake. New York: Heritage, 1940.

Oesterreicher, John. *The Hasidic Movement.* New York: Pantheon, 1958.

Paine, Albert Bigelow. *A Short Life of Mark Twain.* New York: Harper Brothers, 1920.

Selincourt, Basil de. *William Blake.* New York: Scribners, 1909.

Sheed, Frank. *The Church and I.* New York: Doubleday, 1974.

————. *The Instructed Heart.* Huntington, Indiana: Our Sunday Visitor, 1979.

Solzhenitsyn, Alexander. *The Cancer Ward.* New York: Bantam, 1969.

————. *The First Circle.* New York: Bantam, 1976.

Sullivan, Kevin. *Joyce Among the Jesuits.* New York: Columbia University Press, 1958.

Twain, Mark. *Autobiography.* New York: Harper Brothers, 1924.

————. *The Love Letters of Mark Twain.* New York: Harper Brothers, 1949.

————. *Mark Twain's Letters.* Edited by A. B. Paine. New York: Harper Brothers, 1917.

Unpublished personal letters from John Howard Griffin, Raissa Maritain, Jacques Maritain, Yvette Naal, Lanza del Vasto, Cyril Clemens, Martin Buber, Dr. Maurice Friedman on Buber, and James T. Farrell on James Joyce.

Van Doren, Mark. *Anthology of World Poetry.* New York: Boni, 1929.

Wagenknecht, Edward. *Mark Twain: Man and His Works.* New Haven, 1935.

Ward, Maisie. *Caryll Houselander, That Divine Eccentric.* New York, 1962.

————. *Gilbert Keith Chesterton.* New York: Sheed & Ward, 1943.

————. *To and Fro on the Earth.* New York: Sheed & Ward, 1973.

————. *Unfinished Business.* New York: Sheed & Ward, 1964.

Index ———————————————————————